T0127722

Mary's Musings

So Many Blessings

MARY KULA ZOELLER

WESTBOW
PRESS®
A DIVISION OF THOMAS NELSON
& ZONDERVAN

WestBow Press books may be ordered through booksellers or by contacting:

WestBow Press
A Division of Thomas Nelson & Zondervan
1663 Liberty Drive
Bloomington, IN 47403
www.westbowpress.com
1 (866) 928-1240

ISBN: 978-1-9736-3428-7 (sc)
ISBN: 978-1-9736-3430-0 (hc)
ISBN: 978-1-9736-3429-4 (e)

Library of Congress Control Number: 2018908446

Print information available on the last page.

WestBow Press rev. date: 8/8/2018

I would like to dedicate this book to my dear, sweet, friend Margie McCracken who has lived for over nine and a half decades! She began being a positive example to me many, many years ago.

Margie's involvement in church choir and her beautiful solos impressed everyone and touched our hearts. She graciously prepared a delicious meal for our entire church every New Year's Eve. She generously made scrumptious food for our church potluck dinners, too. I admire her wonderful Christian example of always giving and loving, not to mention her words of encouragement. I call her "my little Margie blessing."

After reading my annual Christmas newsletters for several years, Margie kept telling me repeatedly that I should write a book. She said, "You have a way with words." Margie is delighted that I'm giving it a try.

I would also like to dedicate this book to my friend, Connie Sheridan. After Connie received and read a few of my annual Christmas newsletters, she asked me if I'd ever considered writing a book. When I replied, "No," Connie suggested that I should at least consider writing a small devotional. Thanks, Connie.

Mary Kula Zoeller
7/7/2018

Acknowledgments

I am grateful to Karen Bingham, my school teacher friend, for her hours of reading and help with editing.

Thanks most of all to my wonderful husband, Michael. My book might never have reached publication without his assistance. I love you, Michael.

These are the stories as I remember them. Some of my family and friends may recall things a little differently, but I gave it my best shot.

My goal is to make you all smile, warm your hearts, and give you encouragement. I hope you enjoy reading this book as much as I have enjoyed writing it.

Love and blessings to all.

Mom aka Nanny aka Mary

1—Trust in God

> May the God of hope fill you with all joy and peace as
> you trust in Him, so that you may overflow with hope
> by the power of the Holy Spirit. (John 15:13 NIV)

For the past twenty-five years I've written an annual Christmas letter to my family and friends. Several recipients have made comments that I should consider a writing career. One friend even went so far as to suggest that I write a devotional book!

My neighbor, wanting to attend a writing workshop, convinced me to join her. It was fun and interesting. I'm not sure I learned much other than the fact that writing can be very time consuming. I didn't sign up for the second class, however, stating that I *might reconsider if I ever found myself with time on my hands.* That time has come. Perhaps that is why I'm living so far away from family and dearest friends at this stage of my life?

We don't know the paths our lives will take, Father, but if we allow you to be the guiding shepherd, it's going to be a good one. Please strengthen our faith as we trust in you.

Song Thoughts

"Take my life and let it be consecrated, Lord to thee. Take my lips and let them be filled with messages for thee."

2–Joy in Others

Blessed is the people of whom this is true; blessed is
the people whose God is the Lord. (Psalm144:15 NIV)

I'm one of five girls. When we were little, the local preacher drove
almost ten miles to pick us up so we could attend vacation Bible school.
I remember painting sculptures of praying hands molded from plaster of
paris. It was also a treat since I loved singing and learning new songs:
"O be careful little hands what you do …"

There wasn't a nervous bone in my body after memorizing the first
fourteen verses of the second chapter of Luke. I boldly recited my lines
telling the Christmas story. I was in second grade. I even learned the
names of the sixty-six books of the Old and New Testaments in our
Bible Buddies group.

When I was in second grade we moved about one hundred miles so
my dad would be closer to work, but I never forgot the man who added
so much positivity in my life. I ran into Pastor Bill a few years ago at the
Canton Christian Home where my mom spent her final days. Tears filled
my eyes as I thanked him for taking the time to care about my siblings
and me and where we would spend eternity.

Father, we want our light to shine for you as we reach out to others
who cross our paths in life. Please guide our footsteps.

Song Thoughts

"I have the joy, joy, joy, joy down in my
heart, down in my heart to stay!"

3—Trust and Obey

> Children, obey your parents in the Lord, for this is right. (Ephesians 6:1 NIV)

My dad was a good provider and always wanted the best for his children. He was very insistent that my siblings and I wore properly fitted, well-made shoes. Good leather shoes for kids back then didn't have as many options to be cute and adorable as they do nowadays.

One time, just for the fun of it, when I was about three years old, or so the story goes, my mom went against my daddy's wishes. She bought me some adorable, inexpensive, red tennis shoes. I was happy as a bug in a rug.

Needless to say, my dad had a conniption fit when he saw my mom's purchase. Shortly thereafter, wanting to make amends, my mom gave away my cool red tennis shoes to a little boy in our neighborhood.

When I saw my friend wearing my wonderful shoes, I knocked him down and took my shoes home where I felt they belonged. Embarrassed by my actions, Mom and Dad hastily returned the shoes, apologizing for my behavior. I didn't completely understand their reasoning even though I knew I had done wrong in their eyes.

Your ways, Father, aren't always our ways. Grant us understanding and help us to be obedient.

Song Thoughts

"So give us clean hands and give us pure hearts,
let us not lift our souls to another."

4—Choose Wisely

> Walk with the wise and become wise, for a companion
> of fools suffers harm. (Proverbs 13:20 NIV)

The sermon was about raising children, and it included this scripture from Proverbs. Even though it might not fit perfectly in this case, it did bring to mind my high school days.

I refused to listen to dirty jokes. Someone told me that if I didn't let go of my lofty standards, my friends would start calling me "virgin ears."

No one ever did, at least not to my knowledge, nor did I ever regret my decision to hang on to my values. I certainly had plenty of other things in my life that wanted to drag me down, and I didn't need any more.

I wasn't perfect by any means, but when classmates asked me to pray for a relative or for a certain situation, I was surprised. It was a good lesson for me about how my thoughts and actions can affect another person. I was amazed that such a small thing on my part could leave either a positive or negative impression.

Help us, Father, to be strong enough to do the right thing, not choosing what some might see as the easier path.

Song Thoughts

"I'm casting my cares aside, I'm leaving my past behind,
I'm setting my heart and mind on you, Jesus."

5—Always Look to the Lord

> "For I know the plans I have for you," declares the
> LORD, "plans to prosper you and not to harm you,
> plans to give you hope and a future." (Jeremiah
> 29:11 NIV)

Having no brothers, my sisters and I enjoyed watching the boys at our church participate in sports at their school. We attended church camp together for years as campers and staff.

We'd even crowd into my mom's car once I had my driver's license and head to the drive-in movie theater. After the show, everyone crashed on our living room floor to spend the night. They were like the brothers I never had.

Once high school graduation rolled around, one of my church friends decided he wanted to attend Bible college in Kentucky. I had no idea his dad wasn't thrilled with the idea.

He kept telling me that he thought Bible college would be a good thing. I agreed. I had a car, and without hesitation I told him that if he really wanted to go, I'd take him. And I did. Sounds crazy, but who knew that he would eventually become a wonderful preacher.

Heavenly Father, I had no idea that you were using me to help carry out your will. Please continue to guide me always so that I can be your servant.

Song Thoughts

"It's your heart I'm searching for. I want you and nothing more."

6—Special Memories

> Then Job replied to the Lord: "I know that you can do
> all things; no purpose of yours can be thwarted ... My
> ears had heard of you but now my eye sees you." (Job
> 42:2, 42:5 NIV)

I attended a reunion at the church where my sisters and I (well, my entire
family, actually) attended for numerous years. It was such a blessing to
see everyone.

Just thinking about those special people who'd had such an influence
on my life was great. Now the minister, the choir director, the pianist,
the church organist, many of the Sunday school teachers, and the youth
pastor, Mr. Logan, have gone on to their eternal rewards.

One fun memory for those of us attending youth group as kids was
the decision to call ourselves "Logan's Heroes." A very special dad we
called Papa, who also organized the reunion, was able to get us an old
school bus back then to use as transportation to youth rallies and church
camp. We spent a fun Saturday afternoon sanding and painting the bus
lime green. Upon completion, we decided we needed a cool name rather
than only calling it the church bus, so we christened our clunker "The
Heroes' Heap"!

Father, we thank you so much for all those special people you placed
in our lives to help us become who you wanted us to be. Looking back
we realize even more what a blessing each of those people were to us.

Song Thoughts

> "Friends will be there we have loved long ago, joy like a
> river around me will flow. That will be glory for me."

7—Songs of Joy

> I will sing to the Lord as long as I live; I will sing praise
> to my God while I have my being. (Psalm 104:33 KJV)

I loved singing in the junior choir at church and can still remember the words to some of the songs we sang. Many times in my mind, I've thanked that special lady who directed the group of boisterous kids every Saturday morning!

She played the piano for our worship service. She even accompanied our ladies' quartet. As a matter of fact, the group was her idea. She found the songs, helped us learn parts when necessary, and assisted us when we were asked to perform.

I finally wrote a letter expressing my appreciation to her. She was touched by my gratitude but felt she was the one who had been blessed. She has gone on to her eternal reward, yet the love for music she helped instill in my heart years ago still lingers!

Our hearts overflow with love for you, Lord, as we praise your name in song and word. Thank you for those who bless our lives.

Song Thoughts

"Shout to the Lord, all the earth let us sing,
power and majesty, praise to the King."

8—Being Thankful

> In everything give thanks; for this is the will of God
> in Christ Jesus for you. (1Thessalonians 5:18 NKJV)

My mother was a talented lady. She played the bass fiddle, guitar, harpsichord, and keyboard even though she could not read a single note! My sisters and I sang constantly, especially while doing dishes or riding in the car. Mom sang too. She was an expert seamstress, always making Easter dresses, jackets, and back-to-school outfits.

Dad never complained about having girls instead of boys, though he told people he got all his girls trying for a boy! Dad posted an arrow at the end of our driveway, pointing toward the house that read "Al's Harem." Dad often spent time with us. He set up a target. He taught us how to load and shoot a shotgun. We could all swim, ice skate, and play softball better than many boys thanks to him.

The memories remain, but my parents are gone. I wish I had expressed my thanks and appreciation more often than once a year in a card.

We look forward to singing with the angels in glory, Father. Thank you for your bountiful blessings here on earth. Help us to remember to say thanks for our blessings.

Song Thoughts

"Count your many blessings, name them one by one,
and it will surprise you what the Lord has done."

9—Blessings Galore

> Your wife will be like a fruitful vine within your house;
> your children will be like olive shoots around your
> table. (Psalm 128:3 NIV)

I loved watching the Walton's television show! A big, old house full of kids and their adventures were delightful to observe. Being one of five girls, with lots of cousins and oodles of friends, we always had a house full of kids and I loved it. While other classmates bragged and shared what they wanted to be when they grew up, i.e. a doctor, lawyer, nurse, teacher, whatever, I only wanted to be a mommy with a whole bunch of kids!

My prayers were answered and my dream came true. Not only do I have four fantastic children, but God blessed me with fourteen wonderful grandchildren, so far! I'm hoping for a few more, but even so my quiver is already lavishly packed. "Blessed is the man whose quiver is full of them ..." (Psalm 127:5 NIV).

Father, you give us so much. It is almost overwhelming when we count our blessings. Thank you, thank you, thank you. Your love for us is overflowing.

Song Thoughts

"I would like to have been with Him then, when He
called little children like lambs to His fold."

10—Keep the Faith

> So Jesus said to them, "Because of your unbelief; for assuredly, I say to you, if you have faith as a mustard seed, you will say to this mountain, 'Move from here to there,' and it will move; and nothing will be impossible for you." (Matthew 17:20 NKJV)

I lost track of how many times I invited them to church. She had countless reasons and excuses as to why they couldn't join us. I felt as though she planned each response in advance, so she'd be ready.

Deep down I knew it was a blessing that she allowed us to pick up her three boys and take them to Bible School. Why wouldn't she? She knew they were in a safe place and probably having fun. They were "out of her hair" and she had several hours to herself.

Free time can be difficult for a young mother to find, but I grew weary with her constant rebuff. Finally, in frustration, I offered a prayer of resignation! "Lord, you know how many times I've invited her and her husband to church. If you want them to come, then you're going to have to get them there!"

When we stopped to get the boys the following Sunday morning, she came running out to say, "I'm coming too. We'll follow you in our car."

It is humbling to think our faith is so small. Lord, deepen our trust in you and your word. Please help our faith to grow.

Song Thoughts

"Faith is the victory, faith is the victory ..."

11—Using Time Wisely

> Teach us to number our days that we may gain a heart
> of wisdom. (Psalm 90:12 NIV)

It was different years ago. People didn't change jobs frequently, if at all. Dad worked in a steel mill for thirty-eight years prior to his retirement. He had accumulated numerous weeks of vacation, so he would still have pay checks coming in when he stopped working.

A Navy Veteran, stationed in Hawaii, my dad fought during the Korean War. He was proud to serve his country, but he was a homebody at heart. Dad always made plans to travel, yet he hadn't even been to our home since we'd moved. It didn't seem like such a long time, but the seasons went by quickly, and before we knew it almost sixteen years had passed!

Shortly before his retirement my dad became ill. When the doctors said the words "lung cancer," my dad lost the will to live, and our hearts were broken. His plan to come visit us never came to fruition.

Heavenly Father, we pray for your loving guidance. Help us to use our time wisely in ways that are pleasing to you.

Song Thoughts

"Still more awesome than I know, you're my coming King."

12—God Numbers Our Days

> A person's days are determined: you have decreed the
> number of his months and have set limits he cannot
> exceed. (Job 14:5 NIV)

After her double mastectomy, doctors gave my mother two months to live. They did not know who numbers our days! In the time to follow, she had quadruple bypass surgery, mini strokes, heart attacks, and surgeries. For the next thirty-five years Mom had multiple health problems, yet she was the recipient of numerous miracles.

My mother's faith was strong and very obvious to those around her! Smiling, she would say that heaven wasn't ready for her yet, and the devil didn't want her! Not discounting prayers, my young son made the statement, "All the doctors have to do is tell Grandma she can't or won't be able to do something and she'll prove them wrong."

Mom even outlived her doctors. Eventually, at eighty-three years young, Mom went to her eternal reward. Now she has no more pain and will live forever in eternity.

We know, Lord, that all things are in your hands, even the universe. Let this be a comfort to us in our time of need.

Song Thoughts

"Our God is greater, our God is stronger. God, you are
higher than any other. Our God is awesome."

13—Meeting Again in Heaven

> They will see His face, and His name will be on their foreheads. There will be no more night. They will not need the light of a lamp or the light of the sun, for the Lord God will give them light. And they will reign forever and ever. (Revelation 22:4-5 NIV)

It has been about two years since my mother graduated to heaven. Rarely a day goes by that she doesn't pop into my mind. I find myself wanting to call and share things with her, or I'm repeating something she said. Her direction and example are more a part of my life than I realized, and I miss her.

Our lives weren't perfect, nor were they easy, but we pushed on overcoming the obstacles along the way. I thank God for the blessings of the family in which God placed me, biologically as well as His family!

As my sister pointed out, there are almost as many of our loved ones in heaven now as still here on earth! What a blessing that we were raised to love the Lord. We know that one day we will meet again in heaven, and we will be together for eternity.

Father, we look forward with joyful hearts to reuniting with our loved ones and spending eternity with you in heaven!

Song Thoughts

"What a day that will be when my Jesus I shall see, and I look upon His face, the one who saved me by His grace."

14—What Would Jesus Do?

Do not take revenge, my dear friends, but leave room
for God's wrath, for it is written: "It is mine to avenge;
I will repay" says the Lord. (Romans 12:19 NIV)

Apart-time assistant in the church office, I was asked to be the interim Children's Minister. Excitedly, I lined up teachers and their assistants, telling them that it was a temporary position until a new ministerial person was hired.

The children in our church, including two of my own, presented a spectacular Christmas program that year under my supervision. It was pretty impressive if I do say so myself!

When the new Children's Minister arrived and assumed leadership, she took an instant dislike to me. I never understood her hostility and resentment, but it hurt my feelings.

It got even worse when almost everything under her direction fell apart. Compounding the problem, lines were forgotten, and the annual children's Christmas presentation was a flop.

My friend, knowing the animosity that had been expressed toward me, asked if I regarded the disaster with a certain sense of satisfaction. My instant reply was, "Not at all." I only felt sorry for her.

Thank you, Jesus, for residing in my heart. May our actions always be prefaced with the words "What would Jesus do or say?"

Song Thoughts

"Heal my heart and make it clean. Open up my eyes to the
things unseen. Show me how to love like you have loved me."

15—Jesus Knows

> So we make it our goal to please Him, whether we are
> at home in the body or away from it. (2 Corinthians
> 5:9 NIV)

We try to limit family visits and the ten hour drive to Ohio or the even more expensive flight. Yet, I was yearning for an appointment with my favorite cosmetologist, aka my daughter. Plus, the twins had a birthday party, and three of the grandsons had basketball games.

Busy at work, my husband could not take any time off. I was too cheap to buy a last minute plane ticket. I disliked the idea of paying a stranger to do my hair when my daughter's salon policy says, "Moms are always free." I was near tears.

I was feeling pretty sorry for myself, but then I decided to stop the self pity and be brave! The local lady who did my hair was incredibly nice. She was a talented beautician charging reasonable prices. I came home delighted!

Learning the basketball games would continue for a few more weeks, and the party had been postponed, were the icing on the cake! Things worked out better than I anticipated!

Father, may I do better at putting others before myself and remembering, not just occasionally, that my life truly is in your hands.

Song Thoughts

"You lead, I'll follow, your hands hold my tomorrow."

16—Remembering God is With Us

> For I am convinced neither death nor life, neither angels nor demons, neither the present nor the future, nor any powers, neither height nor depth, nor anything else in all creation, will be able to separate us from the love of God that is in Christ Jesus. (Romans 8:38-39 NIV)

I've lived in four different places in three different states in the past fifteen years. I've learned that home isn't just the house in which I live. It's where my heart is. Most people have heard me say that my heart is in Ohio since that's where my family lives.

More importantly, I'm learning that my heart is with the Lord. One of my favorite songs says, "This world is not my home, I'm just passing through."

I like the changing seasons, but once Christmas is over I'm ready for spring! Snow can be beautiful, but two or three weeks of snow are sufficient for me. I'd much prefer a warm, sandy beach.

That might be part of the reason I remember these words I once read. They paint such a visual picture for me. "As the sand sinks swiftly down, be love-led rather than fear-driven, to stand on the rock underneath."

Incredible words to memorize since they describe the faith I want to have. I still face numerous changes and challenges every day of my life. I want to be brave and trust in the plans that God has for me, no matter what my earthly address might be.

Life takes us many places. In our joy or even our discomfort, Father, help us to always remember that you are with us. Help our foundation to be firm in you.

Song Thoughts

"A thousand times I've failed, still your mercy remains, and should I stumble again, I'm caught in your grace everlasting."

17—Words to Remember

> Every good and perfect gift is from above, coming
> down from the Father of the heavenly lights, who does
> not change like shifting shadows. (James 1:17 NIV)

I try to always keep my eyes and ears open for words of wisdom. My bulletin board is covered with snippets of profound thoughts.

Our pastor once said "As Christians, we are like snow. People see the footprints that we leave."

That reminds me of these words I heard someone else say. "We might be the only Bible some people will read, all of Jesus they will see."

Both statements are good reminders to be stuck in my head as we move throughout the world in our daily lives.

This past Christmas while at the Mall of America, I saw a sign saying "Maybe you can live without it but why take the chance?"

Another countered "You can't have everything! Where would you put it?"

Both phrases made me smile, though my favorite is "Jesus is the gift that perfectly fits the size of every heart. Jesus is the reason for the season."

Your gifts are numerous, Lord, so many we can't begin to count them. Help us to lead others by our example, and love them the way you love us.

Song Thoughts

"That's why we love Him, that's why we sing,
'cause He gave His everything."

18—Aging Gracefully

> Gray hair is a crown of splendor; it is attained in the
> way of righteousness. (Proverbs 16:31 NIV)

I turned on the television just in time to catch the interview of a lady who was celebrating her 101st birthday. The emcee asked, "So, tell us. What does it feel like to be 101 years old?"

"Not bad," she quickly responded, "considering the alternative!"

Everyone laughed. I thought to myself "she's still got it!" Should I live to be that age, I hope I can be just as clever and optimistic.

In today's world surrounded by a culture that looks at youth and beauty as standards, where facelifts and hair color are easily accessible, who wants to admit their true age? It was hard to accept that my younger days were a thing of the past until I learned to look at growing old differently. I realized not everyone gets that chance. Once I reached that proper mindset, this scripture was revealed to me. "He renews your youth, you're always young in His presence." (Psalm 103:5 MSG).

Father, increase our love for you as we make a conscious decision to give you control, trusting the plan you have for our lives.

Song Thoughts

"So I'm never gonna stop, never gonna stop lifting up my
hands to you, lifting up my heart ... I'll be praising you!"

19—Remember His Promises

> I lift up my eyes to the mountains – Where does my
> help come from? My help comes from the Lord, the
> Maker of heaven and earth. (Psalm 122:1-2 NIV)

Why do I pray about something and then seem surprised when God
answers? I wanted to share my faith and God's love with two of my
neighbor ladies, but I was unsure how to make it happen. Our church
is about twenty-five minutes away, and I had already told my neighbors
that I thought they'd enjoy the services. They both told me that they
weren't interested.

One of my church friends asked me to join her for an Esther Bible
study, part of which I had already done. I had allowed myself to put it
aside unfinished when we moved. When my church friend mentioned
that she would be missing part of the study during her son's lacrosse
season, I jumped at the unexpected opportunity. Perhaps we could
complete it together. I had the videos, and we both had our workbooks.
We could even extend an invitation to my new friends who lived nearby!

Thank you, Father, for answered prayer even before I ask. Please
help me to always remember your love and your promises.

Song Thoughts

"Light of the world, you stepped down into darkness;
opened my eyes, let me see beauty that made this
heart adore you, hope of a life spent with you."

20—Always Give Your Best

> Whatever your hand finds to do, do it with all your
> might. (Ecclesiastes 9:10 NIV)

"Where did you get all that blonde hair?"
"From mommy."
"Where did you get that beautiful smile?"
"From mommy."
"Where did you get those pretty blue eyes?"
"From K-Mart!" My son knew my eyes were green!

When my son was about ten years old, someone asked him what he wanted to be when he grew up. He quickly replied "I want to be a baseball player! I'll even play for the Cleveland Indians if I have to!"

My son, though young, understood that you had to begin somewhere, and then work hard for whatever you wanted to accomplish. He never became a professional baseball player, but he always gave one hundred percent when playing sports.

He played first base and pitched on the school's baseball team. Perfecting his three point shot, my son caught the basketball coach's attention. He was chosen as a starter for the school's basketball team.

Being the starting quarterback in high school, my son was even offered a football scholarship. After graduating he coached middle school basketball and football for several years. Even now, my son coaches and plays on the church softball team. A naturally talented athlete, maybe, but he has always practiced diligently.

Thank you, Father, for our blessings and talents. Please help us to give each job our best, Lord, working for your approval, not that of man.

Song Thoughts

"Every blessing you pour out I'll turn back to
praise. Blessed be the name of the Lord."

21—Making the Most of Life

Why, you do not even know what will happen tomorrow. What is your life? You are a mist that appears for a little while and then vanishes. (James 4:14 NIV)

My daughter-in-law was due any day now, so when my telephone rang at 5:00 a.m. and I heard my son's voice, the first words out of my mouth were, "We have a new baby!"

"Yeah, but it's not the one you think," responded my son.

He went on to explain that he had been in the hospital after breaking his ankle. He tore some ligaments and damaged his Achilles tendon while playing racquetball with his buddy.

The severe damage required the doctor to place two screws and a metal plate in his ankle. Eventually, once some healing had started, he would be able to get around with crutches. Meanwhile, the doctor's instructions were to stay put and keep that leg elevated.

Needless to say, my son's family needed some help. It was sad to hear the news of his accident, yet I was happy to have extra time with them, assisting wherever I could. I cherish the time I was able to spend with my grandson, his new baby sister, and their family. My heart quickly grew attached to my new granddaughter. I burst into tears the day I had to return home, leaving everyone behind until my next visit.

Thank you so much, Father, for the gift of family and for walking beside us in our times of need.

Song Thoughts

"Day by day and with each passing moment,
strength I find to meet my trials here."

22—Keeping Young and Active

But you yourself will never grow old. You are forever,
and your years never end. (Psalm 102: 27 NIV)

"**G**uess what? I fractured my tibia and tore my MCL at our softball game last night. Another guy and I were both trying to catch the same fly ball and we collided." My grown son shared the news.

He went on to say, "When I called to tell my boss what had happened, and that I wouldn't be in to work today, his response was when do you think that you will remember that you aren't thirty anymore?"

None of us really want to grow old. We want to remain young and active. My son is still coaching the church's softball team, and yes, he's still playing.

Recently, now that things have healed, I think I heard him make the comment, "Well, at least my legs look the same now."

Thank you, heavenly Father, for all your blessings and for each day that you give us here on earth. Most of all we thank you for the promise of eternal life with you in heaven some day.

Song Thoughts

"Never grow old, in a land where we'll never grow old."

23–Joys of Grandchildren

> Then people brought little children for Jesus to place his hands on them and pray for them. (Matthew 19:13 NIV)

Living so far away in a different state, I didn't get to visit my grandchildren as often as I would have liked. I was amazed at how quickly they were growing. They weren't babies anymore!

My three-year-old grandson enjoyed playing inside his little tent set up in the corner of their family room. He loved it when Nanny would crawl into the tiny space with him. It felt kind of like we were alone in the world. Tee hee …

We often played trains, but sometimes he had a new toy or game he wanted to show me. On one visit he impressed me by showing me his new puzzle of America. Not only could he put all fifty states into their correct locations on the map, he would tell me the name of every one of them. I was even more impressed when he showed me where he lived in Ohio. Then he pointed to New York showing me where his Nanny lived, which was very far away.

I like to tell my friends and my grandchildren that they get their smarts from me. Maybe they believe it, maybe not.

Heavenly Father, we love our grandchildren so much. Thank you so much for each and every one of them. Please bless them, and open their hearts to you.

Song Thoughts

"You're a good, good Father, that's who you are, and I'm loved by you."

24—Staying Strong

I can do all things through Christ who strengthens me.
(Philippians 4:13 NKJV)

Most of my grandchildren have older siblings. As the little ones grow they are eager to attend school like the big kids. Not surprisingly, they have no idea what it will be like in school. They don't really know what they will be doing, nor do they realize how long those few hours away from home might feel.

When one of my granddaughters started kindergarten, she felt like the time there was never ending. Prior to starting school, she was accustomed to not really having a schedule for her day. She could pretty much do her own thing.

Starting kindergarten, my granddaughter liked her teacher, and she enjoyed being at school with her friends. Most of the activities were interesting and fun, but she quickly grew weary, ready to go home so she could take a break.

After several days of going to school, even though she only went for half a day, she was glad when it ended. She tiredly walked into her home and asked, "Who signed me up for everyday?"

Heavenly Father, sometimes our days do seem endless and tiring, but thank you for your promise to be with us and to renew our strength.

Song Thoughts

"As the deer pants for the water, so my soul longs
after you, you alone are my heart's desire."

25—Gaining Wisdom

> Turning your ear to wisdom and applying your heart
> to understanding. (Proverbs 2:2 NIV)

During an evangelistic sermon one evening, the minister talked about hell. He emphasized that anyone whose name wasn't found in the Book of Life was cast into the fire. There would be weeping and gnashing of teeth, and burning beyond anything we could even think of or imagine. He said the Bible told us that hell would not only rain fire and brimstone, but there would be chains of darkness. All those things, plus they would be tormented eternally, according to what my young daughter could remember.

Hearing a sermon like this for the first time, she was very curious and totally mystified by the idea of hell and fire. For days she continued to think about it, constantly asking questions. She kept mulling everything over and over in her mind.

I was getting tired of her endless questions. When she finally told me that she wanted to see hell, I frustratingly said, "You can't, there's no way. Once you see the fire, it will be too late. You'll get burned up."

Her calm response was, "No, I won't. I'll stay in the car."

Thank you, Jesus, for dying for our sins. Help us to become like little children, fascinated by your word. We want to know you better and love you more.

Song Thoughts

"Redeemed, how I love to proclaim it!
Redeemed by the blood of the Lamb."

26—Through the Eyes of a Child

> But the Lord said to Samuel, "... People look at the
> outward appearance, but the Lord looks at the heart."
> (1 Samuel 16:7 NIV)

I took my little ones to their Bible School classes every Sunday morning. The children were usually with the same teacher for approximately two to three years. Then a promotion service was held annually for those who had outgrown their current age group. Students would proudly move on to the next level.

Thrilled to be getting away from the wee little kids' class, my daughter happily received her promotion certificate. She readily went to her new class anxious to meet her stylishly attired teacher, a tall, bigger boned woman.

After our adult class, I went to get my daughter. When I opened the door, she was grinning from ear to ear, talking with her teacher while she waited for me. Upon seeing me, she loudly exclaimed, "See my big teacher? See my big teacher's boots?"

I was embarrassed, but her teacher just laughed. My little ones were always some of her favorite students although I'm not sure why. Ha, ha.

***

Father, help us to see people as you do. Help us to look at their hearts and their love in serving you.

Song Thoughts

"Mold me, make me, fill me, use me. Spirit of
the living God, fall fresh on me."

27—Kind Hearts

> The tongue has the power of life and death, and those
> who love it will eat its fruit. (Proverbs 18:21 NIV)

All my daughters are beautiful! Perhaps I am a little prejudiced, but shouldn't mothers be like that? My son is very handsome as well.

My oldest daughter had freckles on her pretty face. I don't even see them, although over the years they have faded. I do remember, however, that she asked at a very young age why she had them! I responded that they were angel kisses! I'm not sure when or where I heard that reasoning, but it satisfied her curiosity. She even sent me a postcard from church camp to tell me that her dorm mom "loved her frickles." I had to laugh. I loved the spelling. I still have the card. Tee hee ...

My daughters were sensitive and initially a little shy as well. After church one Sunday, they were exclaiming that so and so passed them in the hallway and didn't even say hi.

My response was, "Did you say hi to them?" When their answer was no, I told them that someone has to go first. They have never stopped talking since!

Help us to realize that you made each of us unique. May we use our gifts to serve you.

Song Thoughts

"I see a generation rising up to take their place with selfless faith; stirring as we pray and seek, we're on our knees."

28—Accept His Plan for Our Lives

> But he said unto me, "My grace is sufficient for you, for my power is made perfect in weakness." Therefore I will boast all the more gladly about my weaknesses, so that Christ's power may rest on me. (2 Corinthians 12:9 NIV)

I don't really want to live in this state. I utterly dislike being far away from my family. Why is my husband's job here? Why does our house have to be on a hill? Can't the driveway be flat? Why can't I be healthy, having strength and energy like everyone else? These are my questions of the day.

A few years ago, following relocation, I removed a bunch of old pictures from deteriorating albums. Enjoying craft projects, I made collages with the pictures I'd taken of my children throughout their lives.

That Christmas I gave each child a large frame filled with pictures from their childhood. I'll always remember my one daughter's words of appreciation. "If you didn't live so far away from us, you would never have had time to do this." I recognized the truth of her words.

We don't know the plans you have for our lives, Father, but please strengthen our faith, and increase our trust as we accept our need for you.

Song Thoughts

"Here is my heart Lord, yielded and broken, merciful Lord, come and restore."

29—Growing Up Isn't Easy

> Not looking to your own interests but each of you to
> the interests of others. (Philippians 2:4 NIV)

My younger daughter was in first grade and her sister had just started fourth. They liked playing with the girls down the street since they were the same ages. Our families were good friends.

One summer day, their friends' dad finally got the new Porsche he had been dreaming of for years. He was "busting his buttons" with pride, and he asked the girls if they wanted to take a ride. After asking parental permission, they took off down the road.

When they returned a short time later, I asked the girls how they enjoyed their trip in his fancy new car. Without hesitating my younger daughter quickly responded, "I'm not sure what all the hoopla is about. Things go by so fast they give me a headache."

Father, we are so blessed every day. Help us to be wise in the way we act and to make the most of every opportunity.

Song Thoughts

"What a day that will be when my Jesus I shall see, and I look upon His face, the one who saved me by His grace."

30—Reunion in Heaven

> Do not let your hearts be troubled. You believe in God
> believe also in me. And if I go and prepare a place for
> you, I will come back and take you to be with me that
> you also may be where I am. (John 14:1-3 NIV)

A frantic call came from my daughter. "The doctor says my baby has stopped growing. They're going to do an emergency C-section."

By the time my husband and I reached the hospital, our four pound granddaughter had been rushed away for specialized care. Eventually, we were able to see and hold her briefly.

After two days our hearts were broken when they disconnected the many tubes and machines. Our darling baby girl lay still, no longer alive. There aren't words to explain the hurting.

The pain and loss we felt was only made tolerable by Jesus' promise to us. Our precious baby granddaughter is in heaven, but one day our family will be reunited for eternity. Jesus said, "Let the little children come ... the kingdom of heaven belongs to such as these." (Matthew 19:14 NIV)

Father, we know eyes haven't seen, and ears haven't heard what you have prepared for us as we anticipate glory! We look forward to the grand reunion in heaven.

Song Thoughts

"Will I sing hallelujah, will I be able to
speak at all? I can only imagine!"

31–Pray Without Ceasing

> I will praise thee, O Lord my God, with all my heart and
> I will glorify thy name forevermore. (Psalm 86:12 KJV)

My daughter and her husband lost a two-day old baby. They had a two-year-old son and she was now twenty weeks pregnant with their third child. When she called to share her health concerns, asking what I thought she should do, my response was call your doctor. I told her she should pray and I would, too.

I was unsettled when she texted me to say they were on their way to the emergency room. She said they would keep me posted. After praying, I felt a sense of peace, though throughout the afternoon I continued to pray each time thoughts of them came into my mind. Still, I was ready to hop into the car and drive the ten hours necessary to be with her. I was thrilled to hear the final diagnosis that everything was okay with the baby. My daughter had evidently just pulled a muscle.

We praise you, Father, for answered prayer, and we know that even before we call, you are ready to answer.

Song Thoughts

"I'm reaching for you, I'm singing to you, lifting my hands to praise you, lifting my voice to thank you."

32—Jesus is Coming Again

> But about that day or hour no one knows, not even
> the angels in heaven, nor the Son, but only the Father.
> (Matthew 24:36 NIV)

Thanksgiving was over, and we excitingly gathered with my daughter's family to help them put up their Christmas tree. When we finished stringing the lights, and put all the decorations in their places, we lovingly set out the Nativity scene.

My little grandson carefully placed the shepherds around Mary and Joseph. As he put baby Jesus in the manger, he looked up at me and asked, "When is Jesus coming back?"

I tried to make it simple, explaining to a four-year-old that we didn't really have an exact date. I sure wish we did know. Then we could anticipate Jesus' return even more. We look forward to heaven where we will live throughout eternity.

Thank you, Lord, for sending Jesus to die for our sins. Thank you for your promise to come again, and to take us home to live with you forever.

Song Thoughts

"Jesus is coming to earth again. What if it were today?"

33—Laughter is Good Medicine

> A cheerful heart is good medicine but a crushed spirit
> dries up the bones. (Proverbs 17:22 NIV)

I was in town with family doing last minute preparations for my youngest daughter's wedding. Siblings were pitching in to help. Things were busy, chaotic, and somewhat stressful. We were running out of time.

One daughter was going to help arrange the centerpieces. I was ready to head out the door in order to finish up some last minute shopping. I asked my three-year-old granddaughter if she wanted to come with me, or go with her mom.

Placing one hand on her hip, and moving the other to her chin, she replied, "Let me think about it."

Needless to say, when I heard her reply I had to laugh. My spirit of joy was refreshed.

Thank you, Father, for the little things in life that give us happiness. Help us to always appreciate the many blessings that we so often take for granted. We thank you for each moment you give us every day of our lives.

Song Thoughts

"Day after day our God is reigning, He's never
shaken. My hope is in the Lord."

34—Sharing Love and Laughter

> And he said: "Truly I tell you, unless you change and become like little children, you will never enter the kingdom of heaven." (Matthew 18:3 NIV)

My grandson and his twin sister came and spent the week with us. Time passed way too quickly, and all too soon their mom arrived to pick them up and take them home.

Saying good-bye and giving them big hugs, I said to my granddaughter, "Nanny loves you so much. Do you want to come live with me and be my little girl?"

"Yes! Sure! Okay." She said.

I smiled and said, "What about your mommy? She loves you a lot, too, and she would miss you."

She quickly turned to her mom and asked, "Mommy, do you want to come live with Nanny, too?"

We thank you, Father, for children and their innocence. They are so trusting and loving, and we want to become like little children.

Song Thoughts

"Oh, the overwhelming, never-ending, reckless love of God."

35—Number One in Times of Need

> Do not be anxious about anything, but in every situation, by prayer and petition, with thanksgiving, present your requests to God. (Philippians 4:6 NIV)

I didn't hear my cell phone buzzing around midnight, but my husband did. It woke me when he got out of bed in search of my phone, turning on a small lamp.

He handed me the phone, and I quickly answered only to hear my daughter say, "It's past curfew time and Tom's car isn't at work, but he hasn't come home. I've no idea where he would be at this hour. I didn't think to ask what time his shift ended. Worse yet, I drove to Ann's thinking he might have gone there. Her garage door was wide open, but her car was gone. I shut it, but didn't check inside because I was afraid someone might be in there! She doesn't answer her cell phone! I don't know what I should do. Help!"

My first reaction was panic, but then I found myself saying "We need to pray! Let's pray!"

Lord, we want you to always be our first choice, not our last resort. Increase our faith. We praise you, Father, for answered prayer.

Song Thoughts

"You alone can rescue, you alone can save, you alone can lift us. To you alone belongs the highest praise."

36—Time for Me

> Be still and know that I am God. I will be exalted among the nations. I will be exalted in the earth. (Psalm 46:10 NKJV)

For years I struggled with rest. If I took time to watch my favorite TV show or flip through a magazine, I'd feel really guilty. I'd hear somewhere inside me, "Shouldn't you be doing something more productive?"

If I saw something that needed to be done, I did it as soon as possible. Then, if there was time, though usually not, I could sit down and relax. When my multiple sclerosis worsened, and I couldn't fix everything I saw that caught my attention, it was awful.

It has not been an easy adjustment. I still have my days, but I've slowly allowed God to change my mindset about the little things in life. I finally realized that when I pause to rest, play, laugh, or to enjoy a blessing, it is an act of worship. God is in control, and I am not. My worth is secure because of "Whose I am." This is what the Lord says: "You are mine." (Isaiah 43:1 NIV)

Father, help me to enjoy each moment you have given me, to do the things I can and to turn the rest over to you.

Song Thoughts

"In my heart, in my soul, I give you control.
Consume me from the inside out."

37—The Blessings of Friendships

> For whoever does the will of my Father in heaven is my
> brother and sister and mother. (Matthew 12:50 NIV)

Perhaps you're familiar with trigeminal neuralgia which is often called the suicide disease. If not, I'm certain you know of other illnesses with pain and suffering that seem never ending.

At a time in my life when I seemed to be enduring ongoing health issues, my sister asked her Facebook friends in a blanket invitation, so to speak, to pray for me. She was overwhelmed by the eager replies. Twenty-three of her friends volunteered within the hour to pray for me, my family, and my problems! Several people knew me, but there were probably more who did not.

Excited by the heartfelt response, my sister quickly contacted me to share how many prayers were being offered on my behalf. My sister asked for me, but I'm not sure who was touched more. Both of us felt extremely blessed being surrounded by those who know and love the Lord.

For friends and loved ones who surround us and encourage us, Father, we thank you and praise your name.

Song Thoughts

"I can't reach high enough … I can't bow low enough … I can't sing loud enough when I'm singing for you, my Lord."

38—He Sees Our Tears

> When hard pressed I cried to the Lord. He brought me
> into a spacious place. The Lord is with me. I will not
> be afraid. (Psalm 118: 5-6 NIV)

I'd spent a number of weeks suffering from the pain of trigeminal neuralgia, and the doctor had pretty much decided surgery was my final alternative. I was accepting that my prayers weren't going to be answered in the positive way I had anticipated. I said the words, "not my will but thine," but I was feeling pretty sad.

I did not have the energy or desire, though agreed to make sandwiches for an outreach program at church. Determined to be positive, I invited a friend to meet me at church when I dropped off the food. She accepted, telling me that she was excited!

A sweet note arrived in the mail from a friend. She had no idea that I needed to hear a kind word of encouragement! In the course of the day, it was like a key turned in my heart, lessening my pain. As it turned out, I didn't need surgery! I do need to change my focus though, worrying less, trusting the Lord, and making a better effort to put others before myself!

Father, help me to remember to love my neighbor, to not put myself first, and to always trust you. I know that you are in control.

Song Thoughts

"There is no one like our God; we will praise Him ..."

39—Simply Trusting Day by Day

> Before they call I will answer; while they are still
> speaking I will hear. (Isaiah 65:24 NIV)

Thinking it was another week away, my husband offered that we could join the family for a big picnic. I had been suffering from some health issues that he thought would be taken care of in the interim. My condition worsened rather than improve, and the trip was out of the question.

Sitting quietly home alone, I started a note to my friend, Margie, who always encourages me. Then other blessings of support, love, and assistance poured into my mind.

I saw the beautiful faces of the many people who provided a wealth of influence throughout my life. My four wonderful children, their spouses, and my fantastic grandchildren, I have so many treasures from heaven. For the men who served our country, some even giving their lives, I'm thankful. And then I was even more humbled remembering Jesus' death on the cross for me.

Lord, please forgive me for needing reminders of the riches you have abundantly provided every day of my life. Thank you.

Song Thoughts

"Better is one day in your courts, better is one day
in your house, than thousands elsewhere."

40—Pictures of Heaven

> He makes the clouds His chariot and rides on the
> wings of the wind. (Psalm 104:3 NIV)

What a word picture, and even more so for a person with limited mobility! Having multiple sclerosis, there are many physical handicaps, mine being mostly walking difficulties. My legs feel like lead weights, and to make matters worse, my energy level is zilch. I've always been a type A personality, running hither and yon, which makes being incapacitated twice as hard.

Throughout the years, I've been forced to slow down. Now I can listen more easily to things God wants to say, hear things He wants me to know, and try harder to become the person He wants me to be.

Sometimes it takes a lot to get someone's attention. I feel that for our own benefit, God will often allow whatever it takes, kind of as an alert to our need for him. Even so, I don't enjoy having multiple sclerosis, and I yearn for the touch of God's hand and being healed.

Yes, my faith has grown, and I have God's promise of a new body one day. "… Behold, I make all things new …" (Revelation 21:5 NKJV)

Your ways are not our ways, Lord. Help us to understand the ultimate victory that will be ours someday. Please surround us with people who will help our faith grow.

Song Thoughts

"Somebody's knocking at your door. Sounds
like Jesus, why don't you answer?"

41—Loving Others

> Be kind and compassionate to one another, forgiving
> each other, just as in Christ, God forgave you.
> (Ephesians 4:32 NIV)

My shopping times with anyone have become few and far between. However, the past several times I have made the effort to venture out alone, there have been pleasant surprises restoring my faith in mankind.

Since I ride a motorized scooter in the grocery store, people often offer to help me reach an item on a high shelf. The most outstanding act of thoughtfulness happened on a rainy day.

A young man and woman holding a bag of tropical fish were standing with a group of us who had finished shopping. Procrastinating getting soaked, since there was no lull in the downpour, we talked for a while.

When the rain slacked off a little, he offered to bring my car to the door, while I waited with his wife. I could see my car and hesitated, since I had never laid eyes on him before that day. But then I relented, seeing that the rain had let up even more.

He quickly brought my car to the door and loaded my purchases, getting "soaked to the skin." The rain was heavier than I thought. Barely wet, I drove home in awe and amazement, wondering how I could ever repay someone I hadn't met prior to that day for his compassion.

Father, help us reach out and show kindness to others, to love as you love us, and please give my anonymous friend a special blessing.

Song Thoughts

"Open up the skies of mercy and rain down the
cleansing flood. It's your kindness, Lord, that leads us
to repentance ... your favor, Lord, is our desire."

42—The Touch of the Master's Hands

> Keep your lives free from the love of money and be content with what you have because God has said "Never will I leave you, never will I forsake you." (Hebrews 13:5 NIV)

Attempting to give my daughter's cat fresh water, I lost my balance. Trying not to spill anything, I was hanging onto his dish, grabbing thin air. I hit the floor breaking my eye socket, damaging nerves in my ear, and tearing my sinus cavity. Surgery was necessary!

In my weeks of healing I felt very close to God. I strongly sensed His presence through the prayers, visits, and kind words of friends and family.

As for the doctor, I have no doubt that God, the master physician, worked through the hands of my plastic surgeon. As it says in Exodus 15:26 NIV: "… for I am the Lord who heals you." I could not have found a more thoughtful or understanding doctor, not to mention talented.

Complete recovery is still underway, but I know my future is in God's hands and I fully trust Him.

We don't know our future, but we do know who is in control. Father, strengthen our hope and deepen our trust in you.

Song Thoughts

"My Savior, Redeemer, lifted me from the miry clay. Almighty, forever, I will never be the same. Hallelujah, for all you've done."

43—Learning to Guard my Heart

> Above all else, guard your heart, for everything you do
> flows from it. (Proverbs 4:23 NIV)

When I got married, my husband gave me a beautiful diamond ring. As one might say, "He paid an arm and a leg for it." I had never before owned anything quite so expensive, therefore I was extremely proud to wear my ring and show it off.

One Sunday, my fingers were cold, and I lost my ring at church. People told me not to worry, and assured me that I would get it back, saying someone will turn it in.

I had a sick feeling in my stomach. I hoped they were right. For days I worried, trying to understand why this terrible thing had happened.

I continued praying that God would intervene. The answers I kept hearing to my prayers were, "Do not store up for yourselves treasures on earth." (Matthew 6:19 NIV) and "For where your treasure is, there your heart will be also." (Matthew 6:21 NIV)

Christmas was approaching and my husband, bless his heart, said maybe we should start looking for a new ring. As I declined, the phone began ringing. My ring had been found and would be returned. I learned a valuable lesson, one I hope I will remember!

Lord, help us to know you better and love you more than the things of this world.

Song Thoughts

"Merciful Savior, longing to heal and bless, you
will forgive all of my sins if I will confess."

44—Beautiful Friendships

For where two or three gather in my name, there am I
with them. (Matthew 18:20 NIV)

Being one of the few, if not the only woman who didn't work outside the home, I was often the sole person in our neighborhood on weekdays. It was lonely sometimes, so I sought volunteer work at our church to be with some other people.

On days when the weather was beautiful and sunny, I looked forward to getting out of the house. Unfortunately, there were a lot of very cold and snowy days. Those were the times I would wonder why I was even making the effort to go anywhere.

Then I'd remember the warmth I felt as we had devotions together, the way we laughed and talked as we stuffed church bulletins or counted offerings. We capped our time together enjoying something to eat at one of the various nearby food places. The "cherry on top" was being with fellow believers, knowing that Jesus was there with us!

Thank you for your promise to be with us. Give us willingness to give of ourselves.

Song Thoughts

"Come and make my heart your home. Come
and be everything I am and all I know."

45—Accepting God's Plans

> You shall not misuse the name of the Lord your God,
> for the Lord will not hold anyone guiltless who misuses
> his name. (Exodus 20:7 NIV)

My husband and I had the opportunity to live in New York for two years, which sounded exciting. I had always lived in a sheltered environment since church was my life. Moving to a state where only forty percent of the people went to church, and some of that meant only at Christmas and Easter, it was like a different world. One difference I especially noted was the constant use of God's name in conjunction with profanity.

During the next eighteen months, before moving to Wisconsin for seven years, I gradually became bold enough to speak up. I even told my neighbor lady if she used God's name one more time I was going to burst into a song of praise. She laughed, but I know she got the point.

When New York once again offered a job to my husband, he asked me if I would be willing to return. He figured if it wasn't Ohio, it didn't matter if we lived in New York or Wisconsin.

My answer to his inquiry was in the form of a question, "Does everyone still use God's name inappropriately?"

His reply was, "Yes. Maybe that is why we're supposed to go?" Tears immediately filled my eyes. We've been here about seven years now.

Lord, increase our trust in you and the plan you have for our lives.

Song Thoughts

"How great is our God. Name above all names, worthy of
our praise, my heart will sing how great is our God."

46–A Good Provider

> Anyone who does not provide for their relatives, and
> especially for their own household, has denied the faith
> and is worse than an unbeliever. (1Timothy 5:8 NIV)

"Boys and their toys" is a line we often laugh at, at least in our house. When my husband got his new riding lawn mower, he was constantly mowing the grass. The neighbor man told me the novelty would wear off, but it never did.

Now it's the same with his snow blower. We had dustings of snow which melted quickly, much to my husband's dismay. After buying it, he had to wait over a year to give it a try. Needless to say, he was thrilled with the four inches of snow that fell one night.

It's easy to make fun of my husband's passions, but love fills my heart knowing he wants to take good care of us. It is nice to know our grass is cut and the yard looks nice. What a blessing it is being able to easily get up the driveway on a wintry day and park the car in the garage. Watching over his family, and providing for our needs, my husband models his heavenly Father. I know God is pleased.

In today's world, it's easy to feel entitlement for certain things. Father, help us to avoid that mindset, and to show our appreciation. We praise you.

Song Thoughts

"Praise the Lord, praise the Lord, let the earth hear His voice."

47—Looking Ahead to Heaven

> Then the angel showed me the river of the water of
> life, as clear as crystal, flowing from the throne of God
> and of the Lamb. (Revelation 22:1 NIV)

What was I thinking? I agreed to brave an eleven mile canoe trip down the beautiful Wisconsin River with my husband and his co-workers. I have no idea what was going through my mind. My brain obviously conked-out and malfunctioned.

It was a gorgeous, hot, sunny day in August and, yes, I thoroughly enjoyed the water, incredibly blue skies, and puffy clouds. But after eight hours of paddling, I was worn to a frazzle, and brown as a berry. There in the middle of the stream, I vividly recalled my limits as an old lady with MS.

I reached the end of the course with no bloodshed, a lot of sweat, and a couple tears. But no, I'll never do it again unless it's the stream that flows from the throne of God and I have my new body like it says in 2 Corinthians 5:4 NLT: "We want to put on our new bodies."

With a certain amount of human fear of the unknown, we yearn for eternity, yet we know it will be far more than we could ever imagine. Increase our faith, Lord.

Song Thoughts

"I'll fly away, oh glory, to a home on God's celestial shore."

48—Standing Strong

> He will have no fear of bad news. His heart is steadfast,
> trusting in the Lord. (Psalm 112:7 NIV)

She raved about my homemade French fries, so I invited them to our home for a simple dinner. When I put extra fries into the boiling oil, it overflowed catching my stove on fire. As I stood watching the flames get bigger, my friend grabbed a rug from the floor and threw it over the flames.

While I was looking at my black wall, worrying about our ruined dinner, their daughter ran into the house yelling, "She flew over the handle bars of her bike. She's layin' in the street. Her sister stayed with her."

Dinner was forgotten, as we rushed my eight-year-old daughter to the emergency room. We eventually learned that she had a mild concussion. When the doctor released her to go home, he told my daughter, "It will be okay. You can still drive."

As my daughter looked up at him in amazement, the doctor jokingly said, "You do drive, don't you?"

We all laughed, relieved that everything was going to be alright.

Thank you, Father, for loving friends and answered prayer. Please surround us with people that can help our faith to grow.

Song Thoughts

"Trusting Him whatever befall, trusting Jesus that is all."

49—Help in Times of Trouble

Look to the Lord and His strength; seek His face always. (1 Chronicles 16:11 NIV)

My mother and my aunt joined my cousin and me for lunch at the local country club. It wasn't a place we went to regularly, and most likely the only time we'd ever eat there, so we were pretty ecstatic. It was quite enjoyable, and we laughed a lot.

After waving good-bye to my aunt and my cousin, I noticed that my mom could barely walk around the car to get inside her door. Somehow I just knew it was a serious problem, so I rushed my mom to the hospital.

When the hospital took my mother away to be checked, I called my friend who was providing child care for my young daughters. Being the special friend that she is, she grabbed the girls and jumped into her car to come stand by my side.

On their rapid drive down the freeway, she told the girls, "I think we should pray for your grandma."

Without a moment's hesitation, my daughter responded, "You're not going to close your eyes, are you?"

Thank you, Father, for loving us and watching over us. Thank you for our friends and for the power of prayer. You have promised to answer even before we call on your name.

Song Thoughts

"There's a garden where Jesus is waiting, and He bids you to come meet Him there."

50—A Child-like Heart

> All your children will be taught by the Lord, and great
> will be their peace. (Isaiah 54:13 NIV)

Few things are as special as seeing Christmas through the eyes of a child. My daughter was delighted by the tree, toys, and songs. She was almost overwhelmed trying to take it all in.

I watched my eighteen-month-old daughter kneel in front of our nativity scene to gently touch "baby Jeesee," identifying his mommy and his "da da," making the "moo moo" and "baa baa" sounds of the animals. She was truly fascinated by Jesus' birth and His straw-filled bed in the manger, surrounded by animals.

Fast forward one year to hear her query, "Why did Jesus have to go to heaven? I want Him to come back now." Surely this eagerness and acceptance of God's plan is one of the reasons we are to become like little children.

My daughter didn't fully understand why Jesus was born in a stable, or why he went to heaven. Yet she was willing to trust that things are going to be wonderful when He returns to take us with Him for eternity.

Father, help us to remember your words, and give us pure hearts that overflow with love for you and others. Help us to have the open and honest faith of a little child.

Song Thoughts

"I will sing a song of hope, sing along, God of
heaven come down, heaven come down."

51—Ready for Your Return

> So you also must be ready, because the Son of Man will come at an hour when you do not expect him. (Matthew 24:44 NIV)

One summer morning, I told my three-year-old daughter to run upstairs and get dressed, saying, "I laid your clothes on the bed for you."

Moments later she returned without a stitch of clothing, although she had slipped on a pair of canvas sneakers. "Where are your clothes?" I inquired.

"Upstairs," she responded.

When I asked, "Why didn't you put them on?"

She answered, "Because I like to be naked!"

"Well, you're going to have to get dressed, since we're going shopping," I replied.

Undaunted, she lifted her foot up, and said, "I've got my shoes on!"

Oh, for the lack of pride and vanity one finds in the heart of a little child, but a little modesty would be nice! Even so, we can't stop short of our goal. We need to be ready and waiting.

Help us to look forward to the day of your return, Father. May you find us ready and waiting.

Song Thoughts

"Jesus is coming soon, may be morn, night or noon ..."

52—A Strong Faith

> Be on your guard; stand firm in the faith; be courageous;
> be strong. (1 Corinthians 16:13 NIV)

The kids loved Halloween. They enjoyed dressing up in silly costumes, running from door to door, and begging for candy. Going down only two or three streets in our neighborhood provided enough houses for them to collect a sufficient number of treats.

Always thinking economically, we usually found things at home to wear and used make-up to disguise their faces. Occasionally, we'd buy an inexpensive mask. Still, it was always fun to see what the stores had, and sometimes we'd get ideas.

My youngest daughter was about three years old. She was unfamiliar with our usual policy, when we decided to make our annual trip to the store. The kids loved going and laughed while trying on masks.

Her siblings were concerned when their little sister quickly became attached to an expensive outfit. I quietly whispered to them, saying, "We'll let her carry it around," thinking she'd grow tired and put it down somewhere.

Wiser than her years, she piped up immediately saying, "I won't change my mind."

Father, we know you love us. Please help us to avoid temptation and stand firm in our faith.

Song Thoughts

"I shall not be moved, like a tree standing by the water."

53—God Answers Prayer

> You can pray for anything, and if you have faith, you
> will receive it. (Matthew 21:22 NLT)

Before tucking my seven-year-old daughter into bed for the night, I listened to her evening prayers. "And please send me a daddy. Amen."

Hearing her plea broke my heart. I hastened to say, "You already have a daddy."

Being a single mom and trying to do it all, she didn't need to point out the facts to me. Her dad didn't have any interest in being her dad, let alone time for us. I hurried on to explain that mommy was no spring chicken. To make matters worse, I had MS, not to mention that most men aren't looking for a ready-made family.

I ended my explanation by saying that I didn't want her to be disappointed when God didn't answer her prayer and send her a daddy. I encouraged her to keep a strong faith, and trust that God would take care of us.

Less than a year later, I was happily married to a wonderful Christian man. God sent her the daddy that she wanted. God continues to bless us.

Lord, you tell us to ask in faith, believing! Please remove the things that hinder us from trusting you! Give us the faith and trust of a small child.

Song Thoughts

"Even when my faith is small, trusting Jesus that is all."

54—The Innocence of a Child

> Let those who love the Lord hate evil, for He guards
> the lives of His faithful ones and delivers them from
> the hand of the wicked. (Psalm 97:10 NIV)

My daughter was in second grade. One day after school, a boy on the bus was trying to be cool by spelling bad words. He spelled a cuss word and then laughed hysterically at her ignorance. When she said, "That doesn't spell anything," he immediately tattled to the bus driver that she was saying bad words.

Before letting the kids off the bus, the driver yelled at everyone saying bad words weren't allowed on his bus.

My daughter came running home, crying her heart out. She explained what had happened with tears running down her face.

My daughter asked me to tell her all the bad words, so she could be certain to never say them. I'm not sure which was worse, imagining me trying to rattle off a bunch of profanity to her, or the sadness in my heart knowing the world my little girl was facing.

Father, we fall so short of your will. Protect us from the devil and evil things of this world that threaten our walk with you.

Song Thoughts

"Give me one glorious ambition for my life, to know and
follow hard after you. Lead me on and I will run after you."

55—Another Happy Birthday

> For through wisdom your days will be many, and years
> will be added to your life. (Proverbs 9:11 NIV)

It's time for another birthday. It seems like I haven't even been out of high school very long. I can't even imagine I'm that old. Where did the years go so quickly?

Once kids catch on to birthdays and people growing older every year, they seem to be fascinated by everyone's age. After listening to our family sing Happy Birthday to me, and watching me blow out the candles on my cake, my little daughter asked me, "How old are you?"

Not wasting a moment, I quickly replied, "Twenty-nine" and started cutting the cake.

"Wait a minute, weren't you twenty-nine last year?" she asked, bewildered.

"Yes, and I'm going to be twenty-nine again next year, too!" I answered with a laugh.

My daughter didn't immediately comment, though she probably thought her mother was losing it. I'm sure she brought it up again later after she had thought about it for a while.

Father, help us to know and remember that each day of our life is a gift from you. Not everyone gets a chance to grow old. May we live each of our days according to your word and make them pleasing to you.

Song Thoughts

"Learning to lean, I'm learning to lean on Jesus."

56—Better to Give Than Receive

> For we brought nothing into the world, and we can take nothing out of it. (1Timothy 6:7 NIV)

When we arrived to pick her up, Grandma was still getting ready. We followed her into the bedroom as she searched for the necklace that she wanted to wear. The closet door stood open and we were very impressed with all the shoes she had.

"Grandma, you must have forty pairs of shoes!" my daughter exclaimed to my mother.

"I do not. I only have thirty-eight, I counted them last night," Grandma laughingly replied.

While talking to my sister yesterday, she said that her son was just like our Mom. He has tons of shoes but keeps buying more. My one daughter is almost the same, but she buys boots!

My sister and her husband are empty nesters, yet they still have things left behind by their children. We have things from our kids, too. I've started giving them their childhood stuff to keep, pitch, or do with as they please. I say "whatever works."

We laugh, Father, but as our faith matures, we're thankful that you help us learn to store up treasures in heaven. It's also nice to know it's better to give than to receive.

Song Thoughts

"Change my heart, oh God, make it ever new, may I be like you."

57—Someday in Heaven

> Say to those with fearful hearts, "Be strong, do not fear; your God will come ..." Then will the lame leap like a deer and the mute tongue shout for joy. (Isaiah 35:4, 35:6 NIV)

I was exhausted. It had been a hectic morning. My young daughter shared none of my tiredness. Now that our work was done, and the chores were finished, she was more than ready to run and play. Her friends were either napping or gone for the day, which meant that left me, mommy, to be her buddy and afternoon playmate.

After a fairly quiet interim of playing with baby dolls, she still had tons of energy to burn. Excitedly, she suggested swimming, playing ball, taking a walk, or riding bikes. I reluctantly turned down every idea she proposed. My mind was willing, but my body was weak.

I wanted her to understand, so I began to explain my limitations with multiple sclerosis. I ended the sad lament with a positive thought. "One day in heaven when mommy has her new body, I promise that we will run, jump, ride our bikes, and play, doing all your favorite activities until both of our hearts are content."

She accepted my declaration as we curled up with some books. I am anxiously and excitedly looking forward to that never-ending play date in eternity.

Thank you, Father, for grace. We yearn for the day our earthly troubles end, and we are in the place you have prepared for us.

Song Thoughts

"All is peace forevermore on that happy golden shore ... what a glorious day that will be."

58—God Gives Us Many Gifts

> Study to shew thyself approved unto God, a workman
> that needeth not to be ashamed, rightly dividing the
> word of truth. (2 Timothy 2:15 KJV)

Our youngest daughter was a very smart girl and nearing the end of
eighth grade. Come fall she would start ninth grade, beginning her
freshman year of high school. Her dad and I had talked a little bit about
college expenses and possible scholarships. We realized it was only a
few short years until the time she would be leaving home. All too soon,
she would be going off on her own. She would be preparing for a future
career.

One day, just out of curiosity, I asked her, "Have you given any
thought to where you might want to go to college?

"Yes," she quickly replied, but she didn't expound on her answer.

So I asked, "Where?"

Again, with no hesitation at all, she answered, "Harvard!"

Somewhat stunned by her response, I countered, "Why Harvard?"

Within seconds I heard her question in response to mine. "It's a
good school, isn't it?"

Give us wisdom, Father, to choose the high road as we travel through
life using the talents you gave us.

Song Thoughts

"Take my life and let it be ... take my will and
make it thine; it shall be no longer mine."

59—Do Unto Others

> Truly I tell you, whatever you did for one of the least
> of these brothers and sisters of mine, you did for me.
> (Matthew 25:40 NIV)

My daughter and I were thrilled to have some quality time together before she began her high school years. Especially in Paris, while her dad worked. It sounded like a dream come true vacation.

However, having MS, I would need to take my battery-powered scooter to do sightseeing. There were stairs into and out of the subway, as well as uneven levels just to board the train.

Since we were obviously tourists, fellow passengers inquired, "Parlez-vous francais?" We always replied, "Un peu" meaning "a little." After laughing at our pronunciation, they spoke to us in English.

I don't think it was ever the same person, but someone always offered to assist us in lifting my scooter, or carrying it up the stairs. We'll never forget the kindness shown to us and the blessings we received through them.

Help us love others as ourselves, and to do unto them as we would have them do to us. We want to love like Jesus loves.

Song Thoughts

"Holy Spirit you are welcome here. Come flood
this place and fill the atmosphere."

60—All God's Children

> There is neither Jew nor Gentile, neither slave nor
> free, nor is there male and female, for you are all one
> in Christ Jesus. (Galatians 3:28 NIV]

For our youngest daughter's twenty-first birthday, we promised her one more big vacation at daddy's expense. She wasn't picky about the place, though she did stipulate her preference being someplace warm with a beach.

Having never been to the Caribbean, we felt that the Virgin Islands would be a great destination. Our time there included a Sunday morning, thus I strongly suggested we find a church service to attend. At the suggestion of our black cleaning lady, we agreed to try her church.

My daughter went hesitantly, fearing she would feel out of place. There were only a handful of white people at the service, but we were warmly hugged and welcomed by everyone.

The sermon was great. We were familiar with the songs and our souls were thrilled as we clapped and sang with them. We smiled as they hugged and kissed us good-bye, telling us to please come again!

We will definitely return, if we ever have the opportunity. The blessings were all ours. Our daughter even loved it, and said she was glad we went.

Father, we want to praise you always in everything we say or do.

Song Thoughts

"How great is our God, sing with me, how great is our God."

61—Why Worry When We Can Pray?

> Therefore do not worry about tomorrow, for tomorrow
> will worry about itself. Each day has enough trouble of
> its own. (Matthew 6:34 NIV)

My youngest child left the nest. Whenever I thought about her, I worried. Was she eating properly? Did she have time to do her laundry? Is she making the right decisions and choosing her friends wisely? What about sleep?

I knew I needed to quit worrying and trust God. Her grandma would have just laughed and said in jest, "No one can tell me it doesn't pay to worry about something. Everything I've worried about hasn't happened."

I continued to pray every night as my daughter seemed to pull away from needing me, except when she got sick enough to want a doctor. My devotions one day offered advice that I heeded. It has finally given me peace of mind.

I know her faith is strong, and God is going to be there for her even though I can't. My prayer now is not just for her safety and wise decisions, but has become, "Help me understand what's going on in her heart. Surround her with friends who love the Lord."

Father, strengthen my trust in you, and help my faith to be real, allowing me to live each day according to your will.

Song Thoughts

"Water you turned into wine, opened the eyes of the blind. There's no one like you, none like you. Our God is greater."

62–*That's Love*

> But God demonstrates his own love for us in this:
> While we were still sinners, Christ died for us. (Romans
> 5:8 NIV)

Tickled to see that my daughter was calling, I happily picked up the phone saying, "Good morning!"

"I don't know how good it is" was the sad response. "Someone stole my cell phone. I knew I should have put it in my pocket, but I laid it under the edge of my coat for thirty seconds. When I went to pick it up, my phone was gone. I've notified the police, and called to have it deactivated. It's hard for me to believe someone took it. I'm sick to my stomach. Why do people steal?" She rambled on. "I probably won't ever see that phone again. I know it was a lot of money, but I've decided to save up, so I can buy another one."

After discussing it with her dad and sleeping on it, I told my daughter that she could have my phone since I seldom used it.

Her instant response was, "I don't want you to pay for my mistake."

But I replied, "That's what love is."

"For God so loved the world that he gave his one and only Son ..." (John 3:16 NIV)

Loving our children so much personifies your love for us, giving your only Son as a sacrifice for our sins. We are so unworthy. We thank you with humble hearts.

Song Thoughts

"So we raise up holy hands to praise the Holy
One, who was and is and is to come."

63—Guard Our Lips

Sarah said, God has brought me laughter, and everyone who hears about this will laugh with me. (Genesis 21:6 NIV)

Mom loved her grandkids and always tried to maintain a good connection with them, often using humor. The kids loved watching television. They mimicked the line, "Up your nose with a rubber hose." My mom joined their silliness. I rolled my eyes but kept my mouth shut.

I worked part-time at the church office, preparing Sunday bulletins and sending out the weekly newsletter. On occasion, I'd make a brief stop at the church during the week when I had my four-year-old daughter with me.

The pastor thought my little girl was adorable. Whenever he chanced to see her, he teased her about giving him a kiss on his whiskery cheek.

That day he decided to try using reverse psychology, and said, "You can do anything you want to do to me, but whatever you do, don't kiss me."

She stepped forward promptly and gave him a kiss on each cheek!

He immediately started laughing, saying "I fooled you!"

Realizing her mistake, my daughter replied, "Up your nose with a rubber hose!" That made him laugh even harder.

Father, we can so easily be fooled by things of this world. Help us to stand strong in our faith. Bless our efforts. Please help us to be good examples to our children and to all those who are watching us each day.

Song Thoughts

"Now let us have a little talk with Jesus. Let us tell Him all about our troubles."

64–Childhood Dreams

> Sing joyfully to the Lord, you righteous; it is fitting for
> the upright to praise him. Sing to him a new song; play
> skillfully, and shout for joy. (Psalm 33:1-3 NIV)

"**M**ommy, you sing pretty. You should be on *American Idol*," my grandson said.

"Thanks, but why don't you be on *American Idol* when you're old enough?" his mom asked.

"Okay, I will! I'll sing <u>Our God is an Awesome God</u>," he happily responded.

"Wow! That would be great. I would be so proud of you," she said.

"I want to be on *American Idol*, too!" his three-year-old brother piped up.

"Okay," said their mom. "What would you sing?"

"Hmmm ... I'd sing Honky Tonk Badonk," was his excited reply.

More often than not children are very anxious to get involved and do new things. They often surprise us with their excitement and enthusiasm. And they sometimes leave us speechless, unable to utter a word. Yet, God entrusted these little ones to our care. It's a big responsibility and we strive to do our best.

Oh Lord, we're so unworthy. Help us to realize we need your guidance to become the parents you want us to be.

Song Thoughts

"Today is the day you have made. I will rejoice and be glad in it ..."

65—A Thousand Years Are Like a Day

> So that you, your children and their children after
> them may fear the Lord your God as long as you live
> by keeping all his decrees and commandments, and so
> that you may enjoy long life. (Deuteronomy 6:2 NIV]

Somewhere along the line, as children get older, they become interested in numbers and age. If not before, it often seems to happen shortly after children have started attending school. They realize their classmates are the same age they are or within a few months.

Even though they don't clearly understand ages or the passing of time, they become fascinated. Then one thing leads to another and children start talking about their parents' ages! And before you know it, they begin to wonder how old is grandma or grandpa?

One evening the questions began, while we were visiting our daughter and her family. Shortly after our arrival, my grandson ran over and asked, "How old are you, Nanny?"

I laughingly replied, "I'll never tell!"

Undismayed, he rushed over to Granddaddy, and repeated his question. Granddaddy responded by asking, "How old do you think I am?"

Our grandson slowly replied, "Uh, at least ninety?"

Of course, all those listening began to chuckle, especially knowing Granddaddy wouldn't even reach his fifty-fourth birthday for a couple more months.

Heavenly Father, we are so blessed by grandchildren. We pray for your guidance, knowing they look to us as examples.

Song Thoughts

"Let us be a generation that seeks your face, oh God of Jacob."

66—Know the Truth

> I have no greater joy than to hear that my children are walking in the truth. (3 John 1:4 NIV)

It was summertime. A friend from our church and her daughter were having a garage sale. With nothing more exciting to do, my four-year-old grandson, Allen, and I decided to take a look and hunt for some bargains.

It was a busy place. Not finding anything we wanted to buy, we got into my minivan to drive home. Our friend rushed over to thank us for stopping by. She immediately said, "Hi Andy," laughing unbelievingly at his response when he told her that his name wasn't Andy.

Every minute or so, while she talked to me, and he could get a word in edgewise, he would say, "I'm not Andy!" She simply laughed, thinking it was a game, and continued talking.

Finally, she told me that she'd better go help her daughter and made a special point to say, "Good-bye, Andy."

As she walked away, my grandson turned to look at me, shook his head, and rolled down his window to yell out, "I'm Allen, you kook!" I doubt that she heard him, but even so, her mind was already made up.

Father, sometimes we want to shut out the truth, rather than listen to what is being said. Help us to always listen and accept your words in our hearts.

Song Thoughts

"Higher than the mountains that I face, this one thing remains. Your love never fails, it never gives up ..."

67—The Mind of a Child

See that you do not despise one of these little ones. For
I tell you that their angels in heaven always see the face
of my Father in heaven. (Matthew 18:10 NIV)

Each kindergarten student was asked to draw a picture of his family. My grandson happily drew his daddy, mommy, and big sister. At the end of the day, the teacher told the kids to put their pictures into their backpacks, so they could take them home and show their parents.

After school he excitedly jumped off the bus, quickly handing his papers to his mom. With a big smile, he showed her each person that he had drawn. Both top corners of the paper had a picture of what appeared to be a sun in the sky.

His mom pointed to the first circle, asking, "What is this?"

He eagerly replied, "The sun!"

Pointing to the second sun, she repeated her question, "What's this?"

Without a moment's hesitation he said, "That's God watching over us."

Sometimes a picture paints a thousand words. Help us to be mindful of that as we raise our children to know and love you, Lord.

Song Thoughts

"Open the eyes of my heart, Lord, open the
eyes of my heart. I want to see you."

68—One of These Days

> We grow weary in our present bodies, and we long to put on our heavenly bodies ... an eternal body made for us by God Himself. (2 Corinthians 5:1-2 NLT)

When my children and grandchildren come to visit us, we like to check out areas of the northeast we haven't seen before. There's usually a lot of walking involved, so I need to use my battery powered scooter, since my multiple sclerosis makes walking difficult. The little ones like to take turns riding with me.

When we reached the area we were going to explore, my husband and son-in-law got my scooter out and started setting it up for me. My grandson walked over to me and asked, "Nanny, do you still have those same old broken legs?"

We all had to laugh at his description, but it touched my heart that my grandson took notice and remembered my problem from a previous visit. I explained as simply as possible that my legs weren't broken, adding the fact that one day in heaven God would give me a new body.

We thank you, heavenly Father, and praise you for giving us eternal life in heaven ... where all things are new. We look forward to one day being at home with you.

Song Thoughts

"You have my heart and I am yours forever, you're my strength, God of grace and power."

69—Teach Them Well

> Impress them on your children. Talk about them when
> you sit at home and when you walk along the road,
> when you lie down and when you get up. (Deuteronomy
> 6:7 NIV)

The little boys had been playing in the yard, but when things got quiet we had the sneaking suspicion they had headed over by the pond again.

Once they were found, my daughter asked her son, "Do you know what would happen if you slipped and fell into the water?"

"Yes, I would drown." He replied.

"And then what?" His mom countered.

"I'd go to heaven." He answered.

"And I would be sad! You would break your mother's heart!" She barely resisted yelling the words at him.

Responding meekly, my grandson said, "God can heal broken hearts."

Words failed my daughter as she hugged her son and they went into the house.

Psalm 147:3 NIV says, "He heals the brokenhearted and binds up their wounds."

Give us the desire to be good parents, and fill us with knowledge of your word, as we teach our children.

Song Thoughts

"I'm so unworthy, but still you love me; forever
my heart will sing of how great you are."

70—Laughing Together

> Our mouths were filled with laughter, our tongues with
> sounds of joy. (Psalm 126:2 NIV)

Easter was a week away. They always colored eggs, and this year would be no exception. The kids were excitedly clamoring around the table, now that the boiled eggs had cooled and were ready for coloring.

Their mom set out the cups filled with just the right amount of water. She opened the packet containing the six small tablets of dye and dumped the contents on the table. Once the vinegar was added, they would plop in the pills, allow them to dissolve, and watch their eggs turn beautiful pastel colors.

When she reached for the dye, it didn't take long to see where it had gone!

Her son grimaced as stains of color dribbled down his chin. He unhappily explained, "I thought it was candy, but it didn't taste good."

Even though their plans went awry, everyone burst into laughter.

Please help us to rule over sin by praying and seeking your guidance, Father.

Song Thoughts

"Refiner's fire, my heart's one desire is to
be holy, set apart for you, Lord."

71—Staying Strong in Tough Times

In your hands are strength and power to exalt and give
strength to all. (1 Chronicles 29:12 NIV)

It was one of those extremely hot and humid days of summer. Their
dad was out of town and their mom had promised to take the kids to
the zoo. Not wanting to go back on her word, even though the heat was
exhausting, she decided an hour or two of fun might be good for all of
them.

The kids cheered when she told them to grab their shoes and get
into the car! Fifteen minutes later, her son was hopping around the
blazing parking lot at the zoo on one foot. The baby was in his stroller,
while his three-year-old brother and big sister were waiting impatiently.

Sweat was dripping from her forehead as she made a final search in
the minivan to find the lost shoe. Finally in defeat, she said the dreaded
words, "Get back in the car," and they drove home.

As the door opened, the missing shoe could be seen lying on the
garage floor. "Didn't you wear two shoes?" She asked in disbelief.

Her son quietly replied, "I thought I did."

Father, override our shortcomings; you promise growth and good
fruit from our lives if we remain in you.

Song Thoughts

"Your love never fails, it never gives up, it never runs out on me."

72—Laughing and Learning

> Therefore I tell you, do not worry about your life, what you will eat or drink; or about your body, what you will wear. Is not life more than food, and the body more than clothes? (Matthew 6:25 NIV)

My daughter took her sons to buy some new clothes for school. Shopping was not one of the boys' favorite things to do. However, they could use a few new shirts, so why not bring them along to the store. They could pick the ones they liked and would want to wear.

Her older son quickly chose two shirts tagged L/G - Large as his favorites. Following the sales associate, they moved on to another section.

Her younger son shuffled through a stack of shirts and then pointedly looked at his mom, exclaiming, "Why do I have to wear ones that say puny?"

We laughed as the salesclerk explained that the S/P - Pequeño means small in Spanish, not puny.

Father, help us to be less concerned about clothing and all the worldly things that drag us down, but rather our spiritual well-being. Please help our faith to grow.

Song Thoughts

"So I put my life in your hands, I'm yours alone.
Lord, I raise my hands to you alone."

73—Keep the Faith

> And let us not grow weary while doing good, for in due
> season we shall reap if we do not lose heart. (Galatians
> 6:9 NKJV)

My grandson had played numerous sports and done well, but he continued to strive for the one sport in which he would excel. He decided on basketball, promising himself that he would do everything within his power to practice, prepare, and even plan.

He was adamant that he would give his best within every ounce of his control. He left no room for failure. He got up an hour earlier on school days in order to run. He wanted to strengthen his muscles and increase his endurance.

Whenever he had a spare minute, he could be found outside shooting baskets. He was always working to improve his aim and up his percentage of shots made. Unfortunately, he was not chosen for the team. We are still waiting for God to reveal His plan.

Father, help us to be strong, and give us courage to wait for your plan for our life.

Song Thoughts

"When my heart is torn asunder and my world just
falls apart, Lord, you put me back together. There is
hope beyond the suffering, joy beyond the tears."

74—Blessings and Smiles

> Children are a blessing and a gift from the Lord. (Psalm
> 127:3 CEV)

There used to be a television program called *Kids Say the Darndest Things*. Art Linkletter was the host. Here are a few examples that he probably could have used on his show.

When my grandson came home from school one day, he exclaimed, "You are older than my teacher. She's thirty-two. I told her that you are forty, and that dad is twenty-three." I'm guessing his teacher didn't believe either.

His brother said, "I hope my hair never turns blond and curly again, because I'm allergic to it."

After a sleepover at his friend's house, my grandson asked his mom why she didn't come to get him, because he wanted to sleep in his own bed. The next time his friend wants him to spend the night, he instructed his mom, "Please tell him that I am not allowed."

While being tucked into bed one night, my grandson announced that he loved his mom so much he was never going to get married. Not to be outdone, his brother quickly smiled and said, "Don't worry, mom, I'm getting married, but we'll probably still live with you."

Thank you for our children. Please multiply our efforts to raise them according to your word.

Song Thoughts

"You're my coming King, you are everything; still more awesome than I know ... You are more than enough for me."

75—Through the Eyes of a Child

> Children's children are a crown to the aged, and parents
> are the pride of their children. (Proverbs 17:6 NIV)

When my daughter and her family moved out of state, I tried to visit them as often as possible. We would enjoy some fun activities and touristy things while I was there.

Arriving at their home, after they picked me up from the airport one time, my grandson patiently asked, "Did you bring me a new shirt?" Being about three-years-old, he realized that's what Nanny often seemed to do.

Our days were busy and the time passed quickly. All too soon, they had to take me back to the airport so I could catch my return flight home.

One afternoon when my grandson was bored, he asked his mom, "Can we go to the airport and pick up Nanny?"

He thought it was a brilliant idea to brighten his day. That seemed to be where I came from, but no, grandmas don't really live at the airport.

Thank you, Father, for our families, for little children, and for the joy they bring to our lives. Help us not to take one moment of our lives for granted.

Song Thoughts

"Still you make time for me, I can't understand. Praise you, God of earth and sky, how beautiful is your unfailing love."

76—Older and Wiser, Still Smiling

> The Lord bless you and keep you; The Lord make His
> face shine on you, and be gracious to you. (Numbers
> 6:24-25 NIV)

Grandpa took his grandsons to the old historical museum wanting them to enjoy it as much as he did. As they walked the halls, Grandpa pointed out various things and made comments of explanation.

After seeing a picture of a red barn, one of the boys asked, "Are you sure that's the only one? I think I saw one that looks just like it at Walmart."

Further down the hallway, Grandpa pointed to some World War I pictures of men and guns, naming the generals, explaining who had been fighting, why they fought, and the total number of deaths.

The boys were definitely impressed, and one of the boys asked his grandpa, "Are you the only person from World War I still living?"

Father, thank you so much for the blessings of young children in our lives. Their openness and honesty often seems to make us smile.

Song Thoughts

"When our work here is done and our life's crown is won, we'll be in a land where we'll never grow old."

77—Always My Brother

Be on your guard; stand firm in the faith; be courageous;
be strong. (1 Corinthians 16:13 NIV)

My grandson was almost three-years-old. He and his six-year-old
brother were bosom buddies. The majority of their lives, especially
that summer, were spent together. They ate meals together, they swam
together, played games with each other, took baths together, and even
shared a big bed at night time.

Now that he had started school, Tony was becoming more outgoing.
Soon he and a neighbor boy became good friends. As kids often do, they
planned a sleepover.

He gave his younger brother a hug, said good-bye, and headed down
the street carrying his overnight bag. His little brother called out in a
sad voice, "I'll never forget you."

He did not understand that his big brother would return. No one
had explained. You can imagine his joy when his brother came home
the next morning.

Father, even though we don't always understand your plan for our
lives, please help us to be strong and courageous, standing firm in our
faith.

Song Thoughts

"Everyone needs compassion, love that's never failing."

78—Sharing Laughter and Love

> We have shared together the blessings of God.
> (Philippians 1:7 TLB)

The kindergarten students were asked to write about what they did on their spring break from school and tell how or why they enjoyed it. Not particularly excited about the assignment, since his family didn't travel out of town that year, my grandson wrote, "Shot hoops. Fun. Colored pictures. Not fun. Took a walk. Not fun. Went swimming. Fun."

My daughter got a chuckle from her son's paper, and she called to share his words with me. It wasn't anything profound or earth shattering, but it was good to laugh together.

We shared the blessing of having a young child in our lives. It meant a lot to me just talking with my daughter. Like most young mothers today, she's busy raising her family, and being a good wife and mother. She consistently takes time to give me a call and ask how I am doing, often sharing a smile.

Thank you, Father, for all the special things that you give us to bless our daily lives.

Song Thoughts

"Lord of all the earth, we shout your name, filling up the skies with endless praise. Yahweh, Yahweh, we love to shout your name, oh Lord."

79—Proud Mama

> Start children off on the way they should go, and even when they are old they will not turn from it. (Proverbs 22:6 (NIV)

I cherish our precious mother-daughter bond. The love we share as mother and daughter always keeps our hearts connected, even though we're separated by many miles. My daughter calls almost every day just to say I love you. Often times, she will relate the different happenings in her life, or share conversations she's had with friends and neighbors.

On one occasion, she shared that her friend was overwhelmed with numerous problems. She found herself at a loss for comforting words.

Then she said, "So I said what you always say, mom. I told her to pray about it."

Ephesians 6:4 NIV tells fathers to "… bring them (children) up in the training and instruction of the Lord." I'm sure it means mothers, too, but I don't think my daughter realized how much it meant for me to hear her say those words. It makes my heart feel good to know that I did something right while raising my children.

Father, help us raise our children to seek your will for their lives. Give us humble hearts, allowing your strength to lift us up.

Song Thoughts

"Who can grasp your infinite wisdom, who can fathom the depth of your love? I stand in awe of you."

80—Unexpected Blessings

> Who can proclaim the mighty acts of the Lord or fully
> declare his praise? (Psalm 106:2 NIV)

My friend parked the car in the street, since the kids were playing in the driveway. It crossed his mind later that he should move the car into the garage, but leaving it outside one night wouldn't hurt.

Then someone broke into the car and stole his work laptop. How could he have been so stupid? His wife threw a fit and they didn't talk for awhile. Ashamed of her reaction, she made a vow to change.

One year later: He was on his work laptop for personal use instead of switching to the home computer. It froze up. He panicked and bought the $300 card requested for keying in the code that would supposedly unlock it. It didn't.

His wife's first instinct was to freak out. They didn't have extra money to waste. Instead she prayed and found God's way is always best. The company fixed his PC virus.

The next day at work, as he was heading to his office, a lady from payroll stopped him. "I was on my way to give you this $327 bonus check from the company." They were twenty-seven dollars to the good!

Thank you, Lord, for hearing our prayers and answering in a way that we know is a blessing from you. Help us to always respond in a Christ-like way to the difficulties in our lives.

Song Thoughts

"Great is thy faithfulness, oh God my Father."

81—Growing Up in the Blink of an Eye

> Fathers, do not exasperate your children; instead, bring
> them up in the training and instruction of the Lord.
> (Ephesians 6:4 NIV)

She laughed at her husband when their fifteen-year-old daughter wanted to go to a movie with some of her friends. He disliked the idea of boys being part of the group and he wanted to say no. His beautiful baby girl did not need to include boys in her life, yet. His daughter was way too young.

Shortly thereafter, she found herself with tears in her eyes when her oldest son showed signs of growing a mustache. Disquieting thoughts ran riotously through her mind. "My little boy is growing up way too fast. I'm not ready for this stage of life. Where did the years go so quickly? There aren't any girls out there that are nearly good enough for him. It's not supposed to be like this. I knew he would grow up, but not yet. No one ever told me it would be so hard to let go."

Father, we pray our children have been taught well, that they will look to you when they leave the safety of home.

Song Thoughts

"Day after day our God is reigning. He's never shaken,
my hope is in the Lord time after time."

82—See You Soon

> But do not forget this one thing, dear friends: With
> the Lord a day is like a thousand years and a thousand
> years are like a day. (2 Peter 3:8 NIV)

A dear friend of mine lost her husband. To let some of us know about his death, she sent out a beautiful, loving email titled "Finally Home".

Having been in poor health for a few years, her husband knew his time was coming and had stated that he was ready to go. A former pastor, he wanted to die on a Sunday. Not knowing of his wish, though mindful he was a godly man, I thought it very appropriate that he left this world on the Lord's day.

A mutual friend, and his former college buddy, also a pastor, offered special condolences saying the rest of us would see him later today. He was emphasizing the fact that it will always be the first day, since "there is no night in heaven" as stated in Revelation 22:5 NIV. His simple statement makes the temporary separation into something positive.

What an incredible thought to soothe our hearts. We know that one day soon, we will once again be reunited with our loved ones in heaven.

Thank you, Father, for your great love. Thank you for sending Jesus to die as the sacrifice for our sins. Thank you for the gift of everlasting life.

Song Thoughts

"In the sweet by and by we shall meet on that beautiful shore ..."

83—Everyday Miracles

> They were terrified and asked each other who is this? Even the wind and the waves obey Him? (Mark 4:41 NIV)

We had a huge abundance of leaves in our backyard. My husband was very busy at work, yet every evening as we sat at the dinner table, he looked out the window in dismay.

Day after day, he lamented the fact that there weren't enough hours of daylight. He was anxious to get outside to rake or mulch the leaves. He was repeatedly checking the forecast for the weekend, determined to find a way to get the yard work done.

I was less concerned about the yard and thinking more about my husband. I found myself praying that God would make a way to relieve the stress he was feeling. That night we heard the winds strongly and endlessly blowing through the trees.

The next morning there was a gentle drizzle falling. As we ate breakfast, we noticed that not only were the few remaining leaves gone from the trees, but all the leaves were blown out of our yard! The soaking rain would ensure they remained in their new resting spot. How cool was that? God helped my husband do the yard work even though we had almost forgotten to ask like it says in 1 Peter 5:7 NIV: "Cast all your anxiety on Him because He cares for you!"

Thank you, Father, for caring about even the small things in our lives. Thank you, too, for the reminders you send us, and for the miracles we see when we come to you in prayer.

Song Thoughts

"There shall be showers of blessings, sent from the Father above ..."

84–A Little Child Shall Lead Them

> The wolf also shall dwell with the lamb. The leopard
> shall lie down with the young goat. The calf and the
> young lion and the fatling together; And a little child
> shall lead them. (Isaiah 11:6 NIV)

One summer morning my neighbor lady knocked on our door. She asked if my daughter and I wanted to go to some garage sales with her.

Even though she was only five-years-old, my daughter loved these outings and thought they were great! She could take a handful of change and buy some things that she liked for only a nickel or a dime.

We agreed to join my friend, but we weren't quite ready to leave the house. In her impatience to hit the road, our friend yelled, "let's go", adding God's name to her exclamation.

We still scrambled around cleaning up breakfast dishes and grabbing shoes and money.

"You can do that when you get back, c'mon!" she called out. Again, she added God's name.

I disliked hearing God's name used inappropriately, but I failed to speak up. My daughter looked at me, then looked at our friend and boldly said, "You aren't supposed to say God's name like that."

Immediately understanding, our friend apologized, saying "I'm sorry. You're right. I know that, but sometimes I forget. Thanks for reminding me."

Oh Father, help us to be bold and forthright like a child, not worrying about ourselves and how we will appear to others in speaking out for You. Please forgive us when we fall short of your will for our lives.

Song Thoughts

"Oh great and mighty one, with one desire we
come, that you would reign in us."

85—Who Knew?

Don't let anyone look down on you because you are
young, but set an example for the believers in speech,
in conduct, in love, in faith and in purity. (1 Timothy
4:12 NIV)

We were in the car, heading to drop my grandson off for basketball practice. He had jumped into the back seat, scooting over to let his little brother who wanted to ride along with us, climb in beside him.

Obviously bored and looking for ways to amuse himself, my younger grandson began to imitate his older brother.

"Mom, will you tell him to quit copying me?"

"Mom, will you tell him to quit copying me?"

"Stop it!"

"Stop it!"

Sighing, their mom said, "He's a lot younger than you and more worldly wise than you were at his age. You didn't have a big brother who did lots of cool things that you wanted to imitate."

"I knew a lot more than you thought I did, mom. It's just that I love Jesus. I have a personal relationship with Him, unlike this copy cat that's annoying me." He replied.

"It's just that I love Jesus. I have a personal relationship with Him, unlike this copy cat that's … Hey, I love Jesus!"

Father, help us to be good examples for others, to remember there is always someone watching and listening.

Song Thoughts

"I've given my heart to know you, I'm living my
life to show you, I'm reaching for you."

86—Joy in Your Job

> May the favor of the Lord our God rest on us; establish
> the work of our hands for us---yes, establish the work
> of our hands. (Psalm 90:17 NIV)

It was a blustery winter day. The wind howled down the street, blowing snow everywhere. In the distance I saw the garbage truck slowly approaching. It stopped in front of each house, extending its claw-like mechanism to grab each garbage can, then lifting and dumping its contents. As I stood and watched, my mind flashed back to a warm summer day nearly thirty years ago.

My little blond haired, blue-eyed boy and I played in the yard. His gaze caught on the big, noisy truck slowly moving down the street to collect the garbage. I could see the fascination on his face when the man hopped off the back corner of the truck to grab a can. Once he had emptied it, he jumped back on and rode to the next house before repeating the process.

"That's what I want to be when I grow up, mom," said my son, "a garbage man. I want to jump off and on the truck like that."

I laughed to myself at his lofty aspirations of hopping off and on a truck all day long.

Father, help us do our very best no matter what our jobs might be.

Song Thoughts

"Walking with Jesus, walking every day, walking
all the way ... walking with Jesus alone."

87—Abundant Blessings of Family

> Children are a heritage from the Lord, offspring a
> reward from him. (Psalm 127:3 NIV)

I have fourteen fantastic grandchildren. Each child is a wonderful blessing to my life. The thrill of a new baby, fresh from heaven, never ever grows old.

I have nine handsome grandsons, enough for our own baseball team. That obviously means that I have five beautiful granddaughters.

The newest addition to our family actually arrived on her due date. She weighed nine pounds, plus ten and a half ounces. Her mommy said, "Why have a baby when you can have a toddler?"

The excitement never wanes. I have always loved children and dreamed of someday having a big family, though I never, even in my dreams, imagined that I would be blessed with so many grandchildren.

Lord willing, there will still be a few more. My youngest daughter was recently married, and I'm pretty sure that she would love to have a couple of children.

God is good. My quiver is full as it says in Psalm 127:4-5 NIV: "Blessed is the man whose quiver is full of them."

Father, we thank you for each and every child, and all of the people in our lives. Thank you for the numerous blessings you shower upon us day after day.

Song Thoughts

"Today is the day you have made. We will rejoice and be glad in it!"

88–A New Baby, Fresh from Heaven

> Guide me in your truth and teach me, for you are God my Savior, and my hope is in you all the day long. (Psalm 25:5 NIV)

My daughter's due date was approaching. We couldn't think of anything else we should buy in preparation for the baby's arrival. Everyone and everything was ready and waiting.

My daughter and I talked on the phone, as we had practically every day for the past three weeks. Then she hesitated and said, "I know I've been saying this every day, and you're going to think I'm crazy, but I think this is the day!"

She boldly declared, "It just feels different today. Maybe it's the way she's moving, but the pressure feels stronger, and it just seems like the time is finally here."

Not wanting to burst her bubble, yet almost at a loss for words, I finally replied, "She's probably just practicing on how to be a drama queen. And she's waiting for the perfect moment to make her grand debut."

We laughed together and talked about how different girls and boys can be. Not surprisingly, we still had to wait a few more days.

Father, we know your timing is always perfect. Increase our faith as we trust in you, and wait not only for the things you have planned in our future, but for your return to earth.

Song Thoughts

"He has promised He would open all of heaven,
and brother, this could be that very day."

89—Heeding Instruction

> Enter through the narrow gate. For wide is the gate and broad is the road that leads to destruction, and many are those who enter through it. (Matthew 7:13 NIV)

Growing up in the country, my sisters and I had a pony. Even though her registered name was Anita, we called her Caramel because of her coloring.

Our friends thought we were rich, ha, ha, and often wanted to come take a ride on our pony. We were always happy to share and excitedly said yes to their requests.

Caramel was a very smart pony, and she invariably seemed to know when anyone was a little inexperienced, or afraid to ride her. When they climbed on Caramel's back, we repeatedly warned our friends to hold the reins firmly. We always explained how to pull the reins in the direction you wanted her to turn and to definitely keep her away from the trees.

Unfortunately, our advice went unheeded ninety-five percent of the time. Caramel repeatedly headed to the low limb on the cherry tree to brush off the current rider. What could we do or say, besides laugh with them? They knew prior to their ride what would happen if they did not make good decisions and maintain control.

Father, help us to choose wisely, heed your word, and follow the path you set for us.

Song Thoughts

"Follow, I will follow thee, my Lord, follow every passing day. My tomorrows are all known to thee ..."

90—*Love Like Jesus*

> Carry each other's burdens, and in this way you will
> fulfill the law of Christ. (Galatians 6:2 NIV)

I was excited to attend my grandson's lacrosse tournament in Pennsylvania. However, when I saw the distance from the parking lot to the fields where the games were being held, I was overwhelmed. It would be a challenge for me to push my walker across the rocky dirt roads and even through the grassy areas.

When I saw a guy driving a golf cart to take big containers of water out to the players, I decided to ask if there was any chance I could hitch a ride. He kindly agreed, and we chatted as he drove. I found out that he was the football coach for the college.

My grandson's team won the tournament. Yay! After returning home I wrote a thank you note to the coach telling him how much I truly appreciated his kindness. I even threw in the scripture from Matthew 25:40 NIV that says: "Truly I tell you, whatever you did for one of the least of these brothers and sisters of mine, you did for me."

I was tempted to throw in the scripture from Hebrews 13:2 KJV about entertaining angels unaware, but I didn't want to scare him.

It thrilled my heart even more when the coach replied to thank me for my thank you note. He sent me a video and a metallic college emblem to put on my car. His closing words were: "As long as I'm here at the college, you'll always have a ride."

Father, we're so grateful for the people that pass through our lives with such giving and loving hearts. Thank you that they allow your light to shine through them.

Song Thoughts

"Light of the world, you stepped down into darkness, opened my eyes, let me see beauty that makes this heart adore you."

91–Take Two

> Just as you cannot understand the path of the wind,
> or the mystery of a tiny baby growing in its mother's
> womb, so you cannot understand the activity of God,
> who does all things. (Ecclesiastes 11:5 NLT)

My grandson came running up to me with a big smile on his face. Grinning from ear to ear, he happily announced, "Mommy has a whole bunch of babies in her tummy!"

Since he already had a brother, he went on to tell me, "You can have the boy 'cause I want a baby sister." I laughingly agreed that scenario would be wonderful. We enjoyed our time spent together the rest of the afternoon.

A few days later when I visited my daughter and the boys again, it was obvious that the excitement of new babies was still in the air. Shortly after my arrival, my grandson came up to me with a sad face, and proclaimed somewhat bewildered, "Mommy says we're keeping them both."

I had to smile when I told him that it was okay. Caring for twins isn't easy and somewhere down the road I'm pretty sure he probably thought they should have given them both away. But he was a good helper then, and he is still a wonderful big brother.

Father, we don't know what families or friends we'll have here on earth, but we can rest assured that each and every person is part of your plan. Thank you for those special people that bless our lives.

Song Thoughts

"You give life, you are love ... great are you Lord."

92—Spur of the Moment Plans

For He orders His angels to protect you wherever you
go. (Psalm 91:11 TLB)

One day after kindergarten, my daughter came walking home with a
girlfriend from church. I was surprised to see her friend, since her
mother and I had not talked about our daughters having a play date.

The girls were excited about being together and ran off to play. I
kept thinking how strange it seemed. Would my friend give permission
for her daughter to come to my house without checking with me? That
didn't sound like something my church friend would do, so I decided to
give her a call.

She was happy to hear my voice and ecstatic to hear the information
I shared. She was very worried when her daughter didn't get off of the
school bus.

My friend had frantically contacted the school. They immediately
back tracked to the time school had ended earlier. Calling the police
was next on their agenda.

No one had noticed two little girls walking down the street together
or saw anything unusual. Praise the Lord, her little girl was safe!

Thank you so much, Father, for always being with each of us and
watching over us every moment of the day. We praise you for your love
and care.

Song Thoughts

"He walks with me and He talks with me ..."

93—Older and Wiser

> But the wisdom that comes from heaven is first of all pure, then peace-loving, considerate, submissive, full of mercy and good fruit, impartial and sincere. (James 3:17 NIV)

When my sisters and I were little, my dad decided it would be a great idea, as well as very economical, to raise his own beef. He already planted a garden every year, so this would take things one step further concerning provisions for our family.

What dad hadn't anticipated was for us to name our calf, Sally. We had a new pet.

When my grandma came to visit and tried to stake the calf outside for the day, Sally had other plans. Much to our horror, we girls watched as Sally tried to escape, dragging my grandma back and forth across the field about four or five times. Finally the calf gave up, Grandma staked her out, and mumbled that "it would be a good thing once that critter was butchered."

Eventually time passed, and Sally disappeared. However, thanks to Grandma we knew what had happened. When mom took a package wrapped in white butcher's paper out of our freezer to defrost, we knew it was Sally. My sisters and I refused to eat Sally.

Needless to say, my dad was quite upset with us. No more raising cattle for him until we were all grown up and married with families of our own. Then it was great when dad filled our freezers each year with steaks, roasts, and yummy homegrown beef.

Heavenly Father, we praise you that we're given wisdom as we grow and mature. Please open our eyes and our hearts to you, who so bountifully gives us all things.

Song Thoughts

"Praise God from whom all blessings flow ..."

94—A Good Teacher

> And now abide faith, hope, love, these three; but the greatest of these is love. (1 Corinthians 13:13 NKJV)

Growing up, I remember my dad teaching my sisters and me many things. He taught us how to swim and how to ice skate. On the days we went swimming, he encouraged us to gather twigs and wood for the campfire we always built when we returned to the lake in the winter time.

Dad taught us how to play softball as good as, if not better than, any boys in our neighborhood. Many times he spent hours participating in a game with us kids.

Dad showed us how to shoot a shotgun, and how to reload the shells. He set up a target for us in the woods for practice, and even took us to the sportsman club with him, so we could try shooting clay pigeons.

Dad taught us how to plant a garden, and how to drive his riding mower to cut the grass. He taught us how to ride a pony as well as how to muck out the barn.

I never doubted that my daddy loved me. However, I vividly recall that I was twenty-five years old the first time that I ever heard my dad verbally say "I love you" to me.

Heavenly Father, you've shown us how to love others by our deeds and actions. Please help us to not fear saying those words to those we love. Most of all help us to love you. Thank you for loving us.

Song Thoughts

"For God so loved the world, He gave His only Son."

95—What an Awesome God

> The heavens declare the glory of God; the skies proclaim the work of his hands. (Psalm 19:1 NIV)

I don't know if my family could have afforded an air conditioner or not, but I can't remember any of us ever wanting or wishing we had one. We loved the hot sunny days when we could go swimming or play in the shallow creek in the woods.

A few times when our dad said it was too cold to go swimming, I remember trying to be sneaky. My sisters and I poured warm water on the big old thermometer nailed to the side of the barn to raise the temperature a couple degrees, but Dad caught on to us quickly.

One of my favorite childhood memories was warm summer evenings when a bunch of us laid outside in the yard. We spread blankets in the grass and gazed at the zillions of stars in the sky. Sometimes we ate popcorn, and occasionally we caught some lightning bugs.

We never failed to be excited by looking up at the night sky. It was inky black, lit by so many stars, we couldn't count them all. Being silly, we often tried counting, but we always gave up. We just looked at the stars in fascination, while our bedrooms cooled down, and our eyelids grew weary. We eventually climbed the stairs to our beds and fell asleep thinking about stars. Sweet dreams. How awesome it is that God knows how many stars there are, and knowing that He has names for each of them. Wow. Psalm 147:4 NIV says: "He determines the number of stars and calls them each by name."

Heavenly Father, creator of the universe, we're so in awe of you. Your power and might are beyond our comprehension. We can never thank you enough for loving us and for everything you give us.

Song Thoughts

"Will there be any stars in my crown when
at evening the sun goeth down ..."

96—The Mysteries of Life

> He will wipe every tear from their eyes. There will be no more death or mourning or crying or pain for the old order of things has passed away. (Revelation 21:4 NIV)

You might say that I was grandma's favorite since I was her son's first child. I enjoyed all the lavish attention she gave me. I still remember being wrapped in grandma's arms while we rocked in the chair, and she sang songs to me.

If I was at her house when the milkman made his delivery, Grandma would give me the leftover change after paying her bill. I was always tickled to get money for my piggy bank. I proudly showed it off, rather than putting it into my pocket until we got home. My mom suggested that Grandma give a few coins to all the kids instead of just me. Not that Grandma listened. Grandma always gave me extra loving and never stopped making me feel very special.

Most young children don't really comprehend a lot about funerals. They may not really be affected much at all. When I was in second grade, I remember Grandma, my dad's mom, passing away. I wasn't sure why, but it made my heart feel very sad.

When my family was driving to the cemetery following Grandma's service, I suddenly burst into tears. My mom turned to me and asked why I was sobbing.

My reply was, "I don't know. I guess I'm crying because everybody else is."

Father, we don't really know of the mysteries of our lives, but help us to know and trust that all things, both now and in the future, are in your hands.

Song Thoughts

"Sing the wondrous love of Jesus. Sing His mercy and His grace."

97—Try, Try Again

Bring a gift of laughter, sing yourself into his presence.
(Psalm 100:2 MSG)

My sisters and I learned to swim at a very young age. We were proud and happy that we could swim, while many other kids our ages had yet to learn. I wanted my own children to have that same advantage. When my kids were young, I decided to take them to the Y for swimming lessons.

No one ever taught my mother to swim. She often told people that she swam like a rock. When Mom learned that I had signed my little ones up for swimming lessons, she decided that she was coming, too. She was finally going to learn how to swim.

We put on our swimming suits and jumped into the car to go pick up Grandma. When we walked into the Y, we headed to the pool area. My mother hadn't put on her suit, so she headed off to the locker room with her big bag.

The kids and I got into the water so our bodies could adjust to the cooler temperature, while we were waiting for the instructor. All of a sudden, my son called out to me, "Look at Grandma!"

I looked up to see my mother coming out of the locker room wearing a bathing cap, goggles, a nose plug, inflatable water wings, and a pair of flippers. Hearing laughter, yet shocked by the sight, I said, "We'll just pretend we don't know her."

My mother tried hard, but she never did learn how to swim. Instead she adopted the line, "I may not be able to swim, but if any of my grandkids were drowning I'd walk on water to save them."

Father, we thank you for the gift of laughter. We thank you for the gift of family and the love we share with them.

Song Thoughts

"I could sing of your love forever ..."

98–How Great Is Our God

> In the beginning God created the heaven and the earth ... And God saw everything that he had made, and, behold, it was very good. (Genesis 1:1, 1:31 KJV)

When we initially moved to upstate New York, we wanted to become familiar with the area in which we lived. We took mini road trips each weekend to nearby touristy places.

One outing we made was to Whiteface Mountain. The Veterans' Memorial Highway rises as you drive about five miles to reach the summit. Then you take an elevator inside the mountain to the very top. The spectacular views reach all the way to Vermont and Canada. Through the coin-operated binoculars you can even see the skyline of Montreal. It is amazing and very impressive.

Not surprisingly, our pastor had made the trip to Whiteface Mountain. One Sunday in his sermon, he made the comment, "I don't know how anyone could look out from the top of a mountain like that and say there is no God." Me neither. Psalm 14:1 NIV tells us, "The fool says in his heart, there is no God."

Thank you, Father, for this amazingly beautiful world that you have created. Please help us to reach out to those who do not believe in you.

Song Thoughts

"Oh Lord my God, when I in awesome wonder,
consider all the worlds thy hands have made."

99—Listen and Learn

Understand this, my dear brothers and sisters: You must all be quick to listen, slow to speak, and slow to get angry. (James 1:19 NLT)

The smartest, most popular boy in our fifth grade class asked me to attend the annual school carnival with him on Friday night. I was tickled. We agreed to meet at the carnival.

We walked around to check out each booth but kept finding ourselves back at the basketball hoop. Three baskets in a row would win you a teddy bear. My friend tried several times but even though he was a really good athlete, he kept missing one basket. Maybe I made him nervous?

Eventually people began to leave, and my mom came to pick up my sisters and me. On Monday morning when I went to school, one of my classmates ran up to me, giggling, with a teddy bear in her hand. She excitedly told me that it was from Friday night.

I was quite hurt and brokenhearted. My friend had tried so many times to win the teddy bear for me, so why did he give it to her? I refused to talk to him.

Eleven years later, my girlfriend and I started taking walks together. During one of our conversations, I laughingly mentioned going to the school carnival with her husband. I told her the teddy bear story, and how I refused to give him a chance to explain.

The following day my friend said, "Before I forget, my husband wanted me to tell you that he did not give her that teddy bear. She grabbed it and ran. He chose not to chase after her."

Father, we so quickly take offense from happenings in our everyday lives. Please help us to forgive others as you forgive us.

Song Thoughts

"Oh come to the altar, the Father's arms are open wide.
Forgiveness is bought with the precious blood of Jesus Christ ..."

100—Choose Wisely

> Let us throw off everything that hinders and the sin that so easily entangles. And let us run with perseverance the race marked out for us ... (Hebrews 12:1 NIV)

When I was visiting my daughter in Arizona, we decided to take the kids to the Arizona State Fair. They loved the rides.

There were a lot of rides for the older kids and many for the younger ones. My little grandson wanted to go on the bumper cars. He barely met the required height to be tall enough for the ride. Grinning from ear to ear, he climbed into a car by himself and waited for the ride to start.

His mom and I watched from the sideline as he held onto the steering wheel. Not knowing how to steer his car and drive, he continued to go in circles. We tried hollering instructions, but the music and noises were too loud. He couldn't hear or understand us.

Finally, the ride came to an end. My little grandson came running over to us exclaiming, "Whew, I'm glad that's over. I almost fell asleep."

Heavenly Father, so many times we run into things without thinking. Please help us to make good decisions and wise choices as we go through life.

Song Thoughts

"Holy Spirit you are welcome here. Come fill
this place and flood the atmosphere ..."

101—Remember Well

He will yet fill your mouth with laughter and your lips
with shouts of joy. (Job 8:21 NIV)

When my son and his family came to visit us we took them to New York City aka NYC which is also known as "The Big Apple." Before it was the "concrete jungle where dreams are made of..." it was sometimes called "the city that never sleeps." No matter, it is certainly a fun place for tourists to visit.

You can see Times Square, the 9/11 Memorial, Rockefeller Center, the Empire State Building, and the Brooklyn Bridge. And that's just to mention a few places. We tried to squeeze in as much as we could in one day.

Exhausted and heading home, I asked my little granddaughter what she had enjoyed the most. She replied, "The lady in the river," referring to the Statue of Liberty. That made me smile.

My smile got even bigger when my son said, "Everyone had so much fun we're all going to move in with you."

I replied, "Let me know when to expect you."

Father, we're so thankful for the blessings of family. Thank you, too, for the candidness of young children that bring smiles to our faces.

Song Thoughts

"I just feel like something good is about to happen ..."

102—Remember to Rest

> The Lord is my shepherd; I shall not want. He maketh
> me to lie down in green pastures ... He restoreth my
> soul ... (Psalm 23:1 - 23:3 KJV)

It is great having a cosmetologist in the family. She enjoys it a lot and so do we. I wish we lived in the same state but we do not. Even so, we try to take advantage of her talents as often as possible when we're in town.

I can't help but remember the first month my daughter attended cosmetology school. She came home very excited one day to tell us that she had learned how to wash hair. Really? I have been washing hair for years with minimal instructions.

Then she explained that they were taught how to do a five-minute scalp massage. Awww...

It has been said that scalp massages send a person into a wonderland of bliss. I agree.

No wonder it feels so good when I'm paying someone else to wash my hair. After getting my hair done, I'm always ready to take a nap. Now I know why.

Father, we thank you for times of relaxation and restoration. Renew our hearts as we serve you. Praise your holy name.

Song Thoughts

"When peace like a river attendeth my way ... it is well with my soul."

103—Grant Us Wisdom

And Jesus grew in wisdom and stature, and in favor
with God and man. (Luke 2:52 NIV)

When my youngest daughter started kindergarten, I wanted to be sure
that she did well. Following the first six weeks of school there was
an opportunity for parents to visit the classroom. Parents could see some
papers that their child had done.

I talked with the teacher, asking her what I could do to help my
child excel. I even asked what books were best to improve her reading
skills.

The teacher looked at me in amazement and said that my daughter
was already an excellent reader. She went on to explain that having my
child in her class was almost as good as having a student teacher's help
each day. She said my daughter tied shoes, buttoned coats, and helped
with many other things.

When we returned home, I asked my daughter why she didn't let
me know that she could read. Her reply was, "I was afraid you wouldn't
read to me anymore if you knew I could read by myself."

Father, help us to be sure to make time for our children. We want
them to know that we love them, and that they are gifts from heaven
to us. Thank you for the talents you give us.

Song Thoughts

"Just a closer walk with thee, grant it, Jesus, is my plea ..."

"A new command I give you: Love one another. As I have loved you ..." (John 13:34 NIV)

I took my youngest daughter to her pediatrician appointment. Dr. Stroebel introduced us to the young intern that had come to work with him.

When the doctor asked how she was doing, my daughter immediately began to talk about everything that we'd done the past few weeks. She was very chatty.

That's when Dr. Stroebel turned to his intern and said, "There is the average speech of a two-year-old and then there's Annie."

The doctor had to give her a shot. He kindly explained that it was to prevent her from getting sick with things like measles or mumps.

As we got ready to leave, my daughter threw her little arms around the pediatrician. She gave him a big hug and exclaimed, "I love you, Doctor Trouble."

Father, we are so grateful for our children and all the blessings that you give us each day. Help us to love others the way you love us.

Song Thoughts

"Living he loved me, dying he saved me ..."

105—Using Our Talents

> "I have told you these things, so that in me you may
> have peace. In this world you will have trouble. But take
> heart! I have overcome the world." (John 16:3 NIV)

My mom was a very talented seamstress. She could use an item of clothing you had outgrown to measure the material to make you a new outfit.

Inheriting some of our mom's talent, my older sister is also a very good seamstress. She makes blue jeans, jean jackets, and wedding dresses. Actually, she can sew anything.

When we were still teenagers, my sister spent a lot of time one afternoon sitting at her sewing machine. She accidentally gathered the bottom of her blouse, thinking it was the sleeve, and sewed it into the small armhole. No wonder it was so difficult and took such a long time.

When she finally finished and held it up afterwards, I burst into laughter. It obviously wasn't funny from her point of view, but I couldn't stop laughing. Seeing the anguish on my sister's face, I took off running when she headed in my direction. I did not want her to take her frustration out on me.

Father, a lot of lessons are difficult to learn, but please help us remember that you will always be there for us no matter what.

Song Thoughts

"Sound the battle cry, see the foe is nigh, raise
your standards high for the Lord."

106—Having Fun

> There is nothing better than to be happy and enjoy ourselves as long as we can. ... for these are gifts from God. (Ecclesiastes 3:12, 3:13 NIV)

I was visiting my grandchildren one day. We were trying to decide if we wanted to do anything, or just be lazy for the afternoon and lounge around the house.

Being mischievous I started tickling my 17-year-old grandson who is almost six feet tall. I am about five feet four inches tall. He reciprocated and soon gained the upper hand. Intending to stop the silliness I had started, I yelled out, "It's not nice to pick on little old ladies."

My grandson quickly responded, "You're not little."

Sheesh. I realized right away that he did not say I wasn't old. LOL ...

Thank you, Father, for our wonderful grandchildren that help keep us young. They are such blessings in our lives. Thank you, too, for each day you give us.

Song Thoughts

"He gets sweeter and sweeter as the days go by, oh
what a love between my Lord and I ..."

107–A Great Big Wonderful World

He is my God, and I trust in him. (Psalm 91:2 NLT)

We had recently moved to upstate New York. As exciting as it was to see more of the world, it was difficult to leave our family and friends. I made the decision to trust that God had a plan for our lives. Even though I was broken-hearted, I boldly made the statement, "Somebody is going to be glad that we came. Maybe it will be me?"

Some children in our neighborhood were outside playing. Hoping to meet some of our new neighbors, my daughter and I went outside to take a walk. We stopped to introduce ourselves to two little girls further down the street. We pointed to our house and happily told them our names. When I said that we had moved from Ohio, the younger girl exclaimed, "Wow! Is that even in the United States?"

Laughingly I assured her that it was. Throughout the two years we were in New York, the girls became good friends. They loved jumping on our trampoline on a hot summer day. Then they would jump into the neighbor's swimming pool to cool off. What a rough life. Ha, ha …

Time passed quickly and soon my husband's job took us to Wisconsin. And guess what? I was happy that we were given the opportunity to come to New York. As I said good-bye with a few tears in my eyes, I realized that I was leaving behind a little piece of my heart.

Father, we have so many blessings in our lives that we sometimes forget to even notice, or to say thank you.

Song Thoughts

"He's my friend, He's my Lord, oh how I love Him, He's my Father."

About the Author

Mary was one of five girls and grew up in the small town of East Canton, Ohio. She is the proud mother of one son and three daughters, all happily married. Mary has fourteen fantastic grandchildren.

Mary and her husband, Michael, met in Ohio. Michael's job initially took them to New York for eighteen months, then to Wisconsin where they lived for almost seven years.

Although they are once again living in upstate New York, they're hoping to return to Ohio when Michael retires. Mary says 'once a Buckeye, always a Buckeye' plus her heart will always be in Ohio where most of her family resides.

Mary enjoys reading, writing, singing and scrapbooking. She loves watching the Ohio State Football team play every year, too! Go Buckeyes!

Printed in the United States
By Bookmasters